The
Barefoot Mailman

Novels by Theodore Pratt

The

Barefoot Mailman

THEODORE PRATT

FLORIDA CLASSICS LIBRARY
PORT SALERNO, FLORIDA

ISBN 0-912451-32-7

Author's Note

AMONG THE UNIQUE MAIL CARRIERS of all time are the barefoot mailmen of Florida. The route of these men was the better part of a hundred-mile stretch of beach along the wild roadless southeast coast. They found it easier to walk barefoot on the soft, giving sand, and had a special technique for being an accomplished beach "walkist." It took three days each way for the carrier between Miami and Palm Beach to cover his route; he walked nearly seven thousand miles each year, usually under a broiling sun, sometimes through hurricanes. The mail was transported in this way from the very early days until the Nineties, at which time the building of the railroad changed the aspect of life, questionably for the better.

Little recognition has been taken of the barefoot mailmen. The United States Post Office Department has retained no record of them, though in the West Palm Beach Post Office there are six excellent murals, executed by Steven Dohanos, depicting the carriers. At Hillsborough Inlet, near Pompano, Florida, the Lake Worth Pioneer Association has erected a memorial plaque, with the following inscription:

"The Mail Must Go"

In Memory Of
JAMES E. HAMILTON
U. S. Mail Carrier, Who
Lost His Life Here In Line Of Duty
October 11, 1887

Hamilton died mysteriously when he attempted to swim the Hillsborough River, in flood, after an unknown person had removed his boat to the other side. The mail bag and his clothes were found where he left them, but it was never known if he simply drowned or was attacked by alligators, sharks, or barracuda, which infested the water. Hamilton, like most South Florida folks at that time—and the present day—was not a native of the state. He came from Cadiz in Trigg County, Kentucky. In a hand-written account kept by one of the several barefoot mailmen still living, he is described:

"Born and reared away from the evils of any large city, Ed Hamilton, 32 yrs., strong, active, and above all, honest, was ready to undertake any honorable purpose at any hazard."

The factual incident of his final hazard has been used fictionally in this book, together with the casual way Palm Beach was named; The Great Wine Wreck; The Celestial Railroad; the houses of refuge built along the unfrequented coast for shipwrecked sailors; and the curiously contested election held over the site of the courthouse for Dade County, then nearly the size of Massachusetts.

While used essentially according to actuality, they have been employed as springboards, rather than foundations, for an otherwise whole tale of the imagination. Certain liberties have been taken in the story with the strict chronology of events in the section in the late Eighties. This has been done in the interests of better presenting the spirit of the times instead of offering a history. In no case do the characters portray, or are they intended to represent, any actual person or parties, living or dead.

The
Barefoot Mailman

One

WATCHING FROM THE BEACH, Steven Pierton saw the Margaret D appear two miles away in the salt mist being whipped from the wave crests. The fifty-foot sharpie bowled down the coast, sails taut and bending their limber masts. Her low rail awash, she skipped over the sea, treading lightly, dancing on the riotous water and never sinking to wallow in the troughs. That, with her flat bottom and shallow draft, was what she had been built for.

She hadn't been designed for what she now attempted. No boat had. Steven's dark brown eyes, beneath the stiff visor of his faded blue yacht cap, squinted to slits to watch it. He could feel the sweat break out on his forehead as the sharpie, without hesitating, swerved full with the wind and then jibed. She heeled over sickeningly. She seemed to consider capsizing and then decide against it, righting herself like a bobbing bottle.

Still she wasn't through with her dangerous antics. She had yet to get over the bar. She scudded, fairly flying toward the shore. Steven held his breath when he judged the boat was going over the sand that came close to the surface. In his mind he could hear the centerboard hitting, then rasping up into its slot. There was a moment during which the hull itself might strike and bring disaster.

The moment passed, and Steven let out his breath again. The sharpie was over safely.

He couldn't see the Margaret D entering the inlet, whose mouth was hidden by a point of land that jutted out, cutting off the view. But he knew that in half an hour she would be putting in at her dock on the inner lake.

Men said you couldn't do it in this kind of sea, not in any

craft. Steven grinned with relief. The movement of his mouth spread his mustache, lengthening it. He ran a finger along the smooth brown hair covering his upper lip, first on one side and then on the other. The gesture was one of satisfaction and pride. Cap Jim had made it in the schooner.

Steven pushed his cap back, to let the wind dry the sweat on his forehead, then snatched it to a more secure position when it was threatened with being carried away. The March northeaster, he thought, would be one of the last until after summer. Soon the wind would take itself around to a steady southeast trade that would blow until after hurricane time in September.

Steven stood for a moment looking south. There was another cause for pride. The beach stretched, farther than the eye could see, a broad creamy ribbon, dazzling in the strong afternoon sun. On one side of it was the angry lace of the ocean. On the other was a tangled vegetation of sea grapes, beach lavender, flowering Spanish bayonet, and half a dozen kinds of palms.

Tomorrow this would be his, all the way to Miami, officially his as the appointed mail carrier along its entire length. It was a good thing he had just turned twenty-one; otherwise the government wouldn't have given him the job.

Steven lingered on the beach, now for a more practical purpose. Strewn over it was the curiosity shop of the sea, bits of wood, bottles, corks, broken sponges, varicolored shells, great thick stems of bamboo, violet snails, chunks of seaweed to which clung tiny crabs, and sometimes the purple blobs of poisonous men-o'-war with their long stinging tentacles. Giant seeds and huge pods were deposited after being carried from the Caribbean, from South America, some of them brought by the Stream from the Gulf of Mexico.

Instinctively, Steven looked for more valuable objects. The beach was a larder and a source of supply for everything from building materials to sewing machines spewed out of a wreck. The shirt on his back, and the trousers on his long legs, had come in the same way, in the form of a bolt of blue drilling cloth, now washed and faded to a gray like that of a sail. Thrown up on the beach once was a galley stove, ever since used in a settlement house. Last week the sea had offered a barrel of lard, found by the newcomer, Quimby, who was keeping it to himself.

The wind, blowing up only since morning, hadn't lasted long enough to bring in anything of value today. After being sure of this, Steven turned, stepped up on the low scarp cut out of the beach by the action of the waves, and made his way across the reef to the lake.

The path leading from the beach for a quarter of a mile was lined with coconut palms whose heads swayed and bowed in the wind. The sand land was thick with them. A shipload of coconuts had once been wrecked on the shore. The great, profuse growth from them spread up and down and across the reef, where they had been planted by the settlers.

The loud talk of thrashing palm fronds settled to a whisper when they became protected by the others nearer the ocean. A parakeet screeched from them as Steven came out on the lake. On a point of land mostly cleared a dock extended over the water, with a small warehouse built at its end. Facing it on the land was a long, one-story building constructed of heavy unpainted driftwood. Its roof was covered with thatch. And though no other building on this side of the lake was in sight, a wide path through the palm woods led either way to homesteads and the houses of other settlers. Half a mile across Lake Worth the sun glistened on several cabbage palmetto houses that looked miniature in the distance.

Steven stopped before the front of the building facing the point. Above the door was a blue sign with white lettering saying, "Bethune Bros.—General Merchandise & U. S. Post Office." In more freshly painted letters almost as large, as if flaunting the fact, was the added legend, "Palm City, Florida, est. 1887." The latter sign, marking the new name of the town and the date it was decided upon, was hardly a month old.

He heard voices from inside the store, and stepped to the door quietly, to look in. Shelves on either side were piled with goods, bolts of yardage, tinware, packaged groceries, canned food, and stacks of mosquito bars. There were barrels, and opened sacks. A farm corner held saws, axes, hoes, machetes, harness, and several plows. There was a tiny candy counter. A shelf of patent medicines seemed, in proportion to the rest of the goods, overly supplied.

In front of this, and in back of the rough board counter, stood a sturdy middle-aged man clad in a high-buttoned lapelled waistcoat and shirtsleeves held by black elastic armbands. Steel-rimmed spectacles were perched more on the end of his nose than on the bridge. His mustache extended past the corners of his mouth, ending in a droop that failed to make his face woeful. He held a bottle in one hand and explained about it earnestly to a red-faced man standing before the counter.

Steven listened as Doc Bethune spoke, enthusiastically rattling off from memory, without looking at the bottle, the advertisement on its label.

"It will cure a cold as if by magic," he recounted. "Best thing for dyspepsia, indigestion, and sick headache, as thousands testify. A wonder specific for neuralgia, influenza, sore lungs, chronic hoarseness, hacking cough, whooping cough, rheumatism, diarrhoea, dysentery, cholera morbus, diseases of the spine, and lame back."

The red-faced man considered this for a moment, and then shook his head morosely.

Doc Bethune reached in back of him without looking and brought forth another bottle. "Parsons' Purgative Pills are the thing for you," he advised. "They make new rich blood. Will completely change blood in the entire system in three months." He looked about, dropping his voice to a whisper, and confided, "Also cures female complaints."

"Ain't got any," the man retorted.

Doc Bethune brought forth a third bottle. "How about

Pratt's Aromatic Geneva Gin?" he asked hopefully. "An invaluable remedy and certain cure for Bright's disease, stone in the bladder, and—"

"—and all inflammation of the kidneys and urinary organs," Steven finished from the doorway.

The two men swung their faces around.

"Howdy, Mister Durgan," Steven greeted.

The red-faced man nodded.

Doc Bethune snapped his armbands. He peered at Steven above his spectacles and his reprimand could not hide his fondness. "Stevie," he scolded, "don't you go making fun of sickness. Mister Dewey Durgan here has been puny the last few days and needs the best advice."

"I'll take a bottle of that there Pratt's Gin," Durgan said righteously. "I think that's what will cure me. You don't need to wrap it. I'll just take a dose or two outside while I'm waiting for Jesse Paget to bring the mail."

As Doc handed over the bottle and took payment, Steven winked at him. Doc's face twitched. This was recognition between them that Durgan was the only drinking man in the community. He lived across the lake where he had a young orange grove. While waiting the years for his trees to bear he suffered, on occasion, from a mysterious ailment that always called for a bottle of Pratt's Gin. Doc played up to the fiction of illness and Durgan took advantage of Doc's love for prescribing medicines. This way, in a community where it was against the law to sell liquor, nearly everybody was satisfied.

Durgan left the store with his bottle, and Doc told Steven, "We better get at the local mail going to Miami; that way, there'll be less to do after Jesse gets here."

"Cap Jim's going to beat him in," Steven announced. "He's already in the lake."

Doc stared. "I always knew my brother didn't have much sense," he said. "Now I know he's got less, with that sea running out there."

"Cap Jim has sailed his sharpie in everything but a full hurricane," Steven defended him, "and he can keep her alive through one of them."

"He's going to get himself drowned doing it some day." Doc brought from behind the counter a small open canvas bag at whose mouth a padlock dangled to fasten it. He took up a rubber stamp by its long black wooden handle, banged it on an ink pad, and reached for the first of a thin pile of letters deposited in a shallow basket resting on the counter.

"The Margaret D ain't any kind of a boat for the open sea," Doc went on. "I'll like it better when he don't have to make the run back and forth to Jacksonville. I'll like it a lot better when they build the railroad down."

Steven laughed as at an old joke. "Next, this fellow Flagler will be talking of building his railroad line clear down to Miami. What's there to connect here and there for? A hatful of houses here, and the same down there. And all that's between is jungle filled with gators and panthers and snakes and bears. Not even a road, except for the beach."

The older man shook his head as he began stamping the letters. "If the railroad comes it'll do you out of your new job, Stevie. What'll you put yourself at then?"

Steven picked up the letters as they were stamped and put them in the mail bag. "By that time I'll have enough of the walking. I'll settle on my Hypoluxo land and start raising things if they ever decide what's best to grow."

Doc stamped two letters, leisurely, before he said, "You need you a wife for that."

Steven sobered and his gaze dropped. "I'll get me one."

"You ain't got any chance around here, with not a young woman in the place." Doc spoke tentatively, as if on delicate ground. "You ain't even ever had any experience at them, and I don't like it the way that's made you woman-feared."

Steven fidgeted, then asserted, "I ain't feared. It's just . . ." His words petered out.

Doc snapped his armbands. A sad expression came over his face. "That ain't all there is to it, Stevie. I blame myself. It ain't been right, the way Cap Jim and me brought you up, having no woman at all about to learn you their ways."

Steven knew that Doc had lost to another the woman he loved, and never wanted anybody else. "You brought me up just like I want," he said quickly. "I never craved for any better."

Doc, stamping letters, was silent. Suddenly, and for the first time to Steven, he looked old. Steven's forehead crinkled as he tried to think of something else to say. He looked out through the doorway. "The sharpie's here!" he cried. He turned, to start for the door.

Doc stopped him. He was pettish, as if taking an emotion out on an unrelated subject, when he said, "Now you look here, Stevie, there ain't any call to go out to them. They can walk on their own legs and we got to finish this mail."

Steven remained. He watched through the doorway as the Margaret D's sails came down smartly, worked by a small, wiry figure. Another figure, that of a great tall man with a heavy black spade beard, sprang to the dock. Captain James Bethune roared something, the words lost in the wind.

The wiry figure followed him to the dock. This was Gerald Watlington, Cap Jim's one-man crew. A dark-visaged little man, with fair hair and wide-open blue eyes, Gerald was a Conch Cap Jim had picked off a Bahama beach two years before. From his English ancestry, he spoke with a Cockney accent, and neither Gerald nor Watlington were parts of his real name. Cap Jim, more aware of this than anyone else, held that Gerald was the best sailor he had ever known, and that anyone who thought he need investigate his crew's background would have to deal with him first.

Gerald carried in his hands a brown paper package, and as he reached the dock with it a third person stepped from the schooner.

The boy was not as large as Gerald. He looked fourteen or fifteen. A cap too large for him covered his head, coming down to his ears at the sides. His legs were contained to the knees in worn breeches, below which were rounded calves with little hard muscle on them. He stood on bare feet looking about as if frightened, and he wobbled, leaning a little to one side and then to the other as if still holding to the deck in a tumultuous sea. Steven stared at him curiously.

The three came up the dock and into the store. "If ever I seen two that was snuck up on," Cap Jim shouted to Doc and Steven, "it's you!"

"Stevie saw you from the beach," Doc retorted. "You and that Conch are going to get yourself into trouble one of these days with your sailing tricks. And I bet you forgot to bring the medicines I ordered, especially Swift's Specific needed most."

Cap Jim stopped stock-still and grabbed his beard with a huge hand. Chagrin and surprise came over his face. "I clean did!" he exclaimed.

Doc began, "Now that's a fine thing—"

" 'e's got it right 'ere," Gerald said, holding up his package. "Don't let 'im 'ave you on like that." Gerald put the package down on the counter and went out of the store.

"How about the lard?" Doc demanded. "You got it all right?"

"There's something I more than forgot, serious," Cap Jim replied. "Because there wasn't any to be found. Not even in St. Augustine, where I put in for it."

"You're going to hear about that," Doc prophesied. "The folks here are going to let you know about it loud."

"Ain't Quimby give up that barrel of his yet?"

"No, sir, he ain't," Doc replied with heat.

Cap Jim stroked his beard.

"Who's this?" Steven asked. He had been regarding the boy, who stood waiting, hanging back by the door. He had a small earnest face with round gray eyes. For an instant they stared at the men innocently. Then the softness went out of them and they became sharp.

"To help you along on your christening trip as a mail carrier tomorrow," Cap Jim told Steven, "I brought you somebody to take. If you want to. Maybe you won't. This here is Mister Adie Titus. I picked him up when I stopped by at St. Augustine. I didn't get it out of him that he was running away from school until we stood down the coast some."

"A runaway," said Doc.

Adie paid no attention. He stepped forward a little. His eyes were all for Steven. In an anxious, high-pitched voice he asked, "You take foot passengers to Miami?"

Steven nodded.

Adie went on quickly, "Does it cost to go with you?"

"The carrier who had the route before me," Steven replied, "charged five dollars. I expect I'll keep to the same."

A brief cloud came over the boy's eyes. "I got one left," he said. He took it out of the pocket of his breeches with a slim darting hand, backing up his statement with the heavy shiny coin.

Steven studied him. "If you can prove yourself, you're only about a dollar's worth."

"I can prove myself." The boy was eager now. "I got folks in Miami. They put me in a school while they started a homestead. I had a letter saying my mother's sick." With a rush he finished, "I want to get to her and I didn't like it at the school."

"I met your folks once," Steven told him. "Heard your ma was poorly. I never knew they had you. But you can come."

"Wait a minute, Stevie, wait a minute," Doc interrupted. He came out from behind the counter to examine and ask the boy, "Did your folks tell you to come?"

The boy looked down. "Not right out."

"And the school didn't know you went?"

"I left a letter."

Doc shook his head at Steven. "You might get yourself in trouble taking him. You don't want to do that your first trip."

Doubt came to Steven. "He can't stay here," he pointed out.

"I'll take him back to St. Augustine if you want," Cap Jim offered.

Adie looked scared. He gazed at Steven appealingly. His eyes filled and it appeared as if he might cry, but he winked back the tears.

Steven remembered another boy. He saw himself at just about the same age, brought here and dumped on the land in much the same way. When yellow fever had broken out in Jacksonville the city was quarantined. Terrified, the populace still tried to get out. The routes north and west and most of those south were effectively barricaded. His father and mother had managed to smuggle him on a boat going south. They remained behind and were mortally stricken with the thousands of others. The explosions from the shooting of cannon, believed to stop the plague, which had done his parents no good, still sometimes rang in Steven's ears.

"It looks to me," he said of Adie, "he's got the right to do what he wants."

"He could say what he does without it being true," Doc warned.

"He might be from some place else," Cap Jim said. "He might have done something."

"It don't look good to me," Doc argued. "He might even be in with them beachcombers living down the line on your route. They're going to do something to the mail one of these days, like I always said. This boy could be part of some trick."

"I don't know any beachcombers," Adie protested. "I've never been here before."

"His clothes never looked to me like they come from a school," Cap Jim pronounced.

"If I dressed any other way," Adie said miserably, "they'd have known where I came from. You said I was a good sailor," he pointed out, as if this might be a recommendation.

"Good sailors ain't always good people." Cap Jim indicated

Gerald, who just then returned to the store carrying a wooden goods box. "Look at him."

Gerald put down the box and advised Steven, "I wouldn't 'ave no thing to do with 'im. There's some thing queer abawt 'im." He strode out again, back to the sharpie.

Steven, while Adie gazed at him with forlorn hope, saw himself again. The people on the boat, after being paid, had promised to take care of him. Instead, they left him on the dock of the Bethune Brothers. When the people here learned from where he came they wanted to send him back. But Doc, and Cap Jim himself, wouldn't have it. They put him in a cabbage house by himself, and brought him food and talked with him from outside. Doc passed in a vile mixture to take three times a day to ward off the fever. Later he was angry when Steven confessed he had poured it through a crack in the floor. Doc had been boasting that he had cured yellow fever. But Doc's anger had passed.

Steven glanced at the boy again. He could see no guile there. But sometimes you couldn't tell. Almost gruffly, he demanded of Adie, "You promise not to do anything against me?"

Light leaped into the boy's eyes. "Yes, sir, I promise."

"Then you can come."

Doc protested, "You're making a mistake."

"You sure you ain't, Steve?" Cap Jim wanted to know.

Steven said, a little stiffly, "Not any more than the time you both took me in."

Doc looked startled. After an instant Cap Jim roared, "By the Eternal King! Whatever happens, you're doing right!"

Two

PEOPLE WERE ARRIVING for their mail when Steven led Adie down the hallway at the rear of the store. The partitions rose high, to the roof, touching the palmetto thatch there, which chattered in the wind.

Steven stopped before one of the doors. "Here's where you can stay tonight," he told the boy.

He opened the door, and Adie peeked inside. The room held a narrow cot, a chest of drawers, and several chairs. There was a single window. It was Cap Jim's room, never used by him because he preferred keeping to the Margaret D.

Adie looked tremulous, almost a little sick. "I can sleep here," he asked, "for the dollar, too?"

"Don't you worry about that."

The boy raised his eyes. They were clear and full of gratitude now. "I got to thank you," he said softly. Then he went into the room and closed the door after him.

Steven was surprised. He hadn't expected the boy to do that. He had planned to show him other facilities, and talk with him a little.

He stood, musing. It occurred to him that Adie must be tired, dog-tired after the trip in the sharpie. Yet that didn't seem altogether enough reason to act the way he had.

He heard a shout outside, then his name being called. It was Jesse, back from Jupiter with the northern mail.

Steven hurried to the store. A dozen men and women were there. He reached it just as a short, dumpy, barrel-shaped man strode in.

Jesse whooped when he saw Steven. In his hands he held a padlocked mail bag like the one resting on the counter. He pitched it at Steven. It struck him on the chest and he grabbed it, clasping it to him.

"It's all yours now!" Jesse yelled.

"That ain't any way to treat the mail," Steven lectured him.

"The way I'm treating it," Jesse cried, "is only that eighteen miles to Jupiter and back. You get it the rest of the way to Miami after this." He turned to the crowd and announced, as if not being able to hold back important news:

"I'll be here most of the week. I'll see my wife for once more than a day at a time." He pretended to glare around at the people in the store as if for someone to challenge his statements.

One of the men spoke up. "Never saw anybody who wanted to be with his wife so much. Even if she is brand-new."

Jesse seized eagerly on this comment. "If you had her and knew what to do," he retorted, "you'd get to her faster'n I'm going this minute."

He turned and ran out of the store on his short fat legs. Good-natured hoots followed him. A woman clucked her tongue with shocked censure.

Doc unlocked the mail bag Jesse had brought, dumped out the letters and several dozen thin rolled newspapers. He told Steven, "You hand it out while I wait on folks."

Steven went behind the counter. He greeted the people who stepped up for their mail. More of them came in. A number commented on his taking over the main part of Jesse's route to Miami. Steven found that it gave him something of a status. It obtained, properly, no deference from his friends, but they expressed a certain aware acknowledgment that he was grown up and had found his place in the scheme of things.

Above his own conversation, he heard other comments. He could pick out the different accents from various parts of the country. Following the Indian and Civil wars, the southeast coast of Florida was opening up. Word had gone out about its richness and its climate, and folks came from many sections for their health, to find a new land, to farm during the depths of winter when things could be raised nowhere else.

"Pineapples is the thing here. Citrus? Truck vegetables? Well, maybe. But let me tell you: ten thousand pineapple plants can be put on one acre of ground to return as much as two thousand dollars a year." That was straight Middle West twang, probably from Illinois.

"My land!" a woman exclaimed. "Mary says Constance has had her baby, a boy, and it got to thirty-two below last winter. She can't believe it was like summer here." That was nasal New England.

"I can't say this country is what I was told it was in New York, but it's cured my lumbago, and I guess anything is worth that, bugs and all."

". . . and he says, 'I dislike to go to Washington City for fear I will be taken for a member of Congress.'"

Steven looked up at the laughter greeting the last remark. He saw Dewey Durgan, the moroseness gone from his red face, his back pocket bulging. Durgan whispered to a group of men surrounding him. "Have a smile with me," he invited. The men looked about furtively. Cap Jim and another man went with Durgan when he strode out of the store.

Deacon and Mrs. Thomas came in as they went out. Steven whispered to Doc, "The Colic House."

"Now you look here," Doc scolded, "it ain't anything to do running down the only boardinghouse we got. Maybe the Thomas House don't serve meals like in a big city, but they don't give you the colic. That is," he amended, "not every time."

The entrance of the Thomases created a stir in the store. Most of the women were clad in plain cotton or calico, their dresses neat but pretending to not much more style than a Mother Hubbard. They looked at the woman who came in with envy mixed with the conviction that airs were being put on.

Mrs. Thomas was a large woman. She gave the impression

that she was armored beneath her heavy stiff taffeta dress; and when she moved, her petticoats rustled and swished. She arrived before Steven like a battleship bent upon destruction, demanded her mail, received it, and moved a little away to open it.

The Deacon, as if receiving permission, took her place. Perpetually clad in a black shiny suit because he had been a deacon in his church back home in North Dakota, he was the nearest thing to a minister for nearly two hundred miles in any direction. He performed the duties of one at Palm City for what flock he could gather every Sunday morning at the Thomas House. There was some question about how married were the several couples whose knot he tied, but the Deacon said his ceremonies in North Dakota had always worked and there was no reason they shouldn't take here.

In a mild, hesitant tone he told Steven, "I always say, a connection like yours with the government, or the church, is the best thing for a young man. It's steady. Especially when he sets about to gather to himself a family as some day you will do, Steven."

"I reckon so, Deacon," Steven replied.

The Deacon, having delivered himself of this, stepped back near his wife to receive from her at second-hand the news contained in their mail.

Complaints about there being no lard flowered into indignation when Cap Jim returned inside with Durgan. Shortening was sorely needed. Cooking could not be done properly without it. Cap Jim hadn't brought it on a previous trip, and now he was berated for not bringing it today. He ducked back at the assaults of the women. His explanations sounded only like excuses to them.

One by one they gave Cap Jim their opinions, and then marched out. Doc chuckled and Gerald, who stood about listening, made curious sounds of delight at Cap Jim's discomfiture. He attended carefully when Mrs. Thomas expressed her feelings. Towering as tall as Cap Jim, she informed him:

"We're not getting proper service in this store, and you're responsible for it. If you can't do it any other way, then you must teach this man Quimby our ways. I expect you to see to this, Captain Bethune."

Cap Jim quailed before the woman, saying nothing. Mrs. Thomas, leaving the Deacon behind, steamed out of the store, her skirts swishing and crackling.

Dewey Durgan observed, "Sounds like thirteen puppies in a fodder stack, don't she?"

Someone cackled. Several of the men left in the store made shushing sounds at Durgan. The Deacon appeared not to hear.

There was silence for a moment. Cap Jim stood stroking his beard. "I expect she's right," he decided. "We got to do something about Quimby. And I think, Steve, you're the one to do it."

Steven stood still. He looked at Cap Jim and at the faces regarding him. He said, "I don't know as I feel mad enough at him for that."

"It would be about even," Cap Jim observed. "Quimby's a little bigger than you, maybe, but that way he wouldn't have anything to call unfair."

"Are you sure," the Deacon piped querulously, "there should be violence about it? Couldn't—?"

"We already talked and argued ourselves blue in the face with Quimby," Doc said. "I ain't for fighting either—especially when we're asking Stevie to do it—but when that's the only way, it's the only way."

"Let me get at 'im," Gerald offered.

"We don't want him killed," Cap Jim growled. "We only want him learned."

"I ain't seen a good fight in a coon's age," a man said. "You think you can lick him, Steve?"

Steven felt more angry at the man than he did at Quimby. "What would you think if you was doing the fighting and I asked you?" The man subsided. Steven had been thinking, and recollecting something about Quimby. "I ain't so sure he's got to be fought, but I'll do it if you want. First I mean to try something else. Quimby's more interested in making himself a meat safe right now instead of giving us lard."

"Which he don't know anything about making," Doc said scathingly. "At least he ain't been in for any sulphur for it. I see what you got in mind, Stevie. But it won't work."

"It can be tried," Steven said. "You let me have a handful of sulphur. Maybe I'll trade it for a barrel of lard. Maybe I won't."

"You do it," Durgan challenged, "and I'll sign the petition the Deacon means to get up for the November election to keep liquor from being sold in the whole county."

"I'll hold you to that," Steven told him. He addressed Cap Jim and the rest of the men. "I'm going alone. Anybody else there would only rile him and spoil the chance of making him see things straight. So you keep away even if it comes to fists."

"Sure, Steve, sure," Cap Jim assured him. "I'll watch them."

The men looked down, and several of them murmured. Doc measured out a few ounces of powdered yellow sulphur and made a packet of it. Putting this in his pocket, Steven left the store and started out for Quimby's.

He accepted without question his appointed responsibility to deal with the man. He didn't look forward to fighting, for he still felt no real anger. But if everything else failed, it followed that someone should do it. It was his civic duty.

Steven took the path north along the lake front. Half a mile on, Edward Quimby had established himself in an abandoned cabbage shack. Quimby had come down from Titusville to Palm City to lead a lonely, standoffish life. Dour and uncommunicative, he was a strapping young fellow with a shock of blond hair. Every week this bleached out more than ever under the sun, until his hair threatened to become white before its time.

Steven came to a clump of bamboo in whose shade the barrel of lard stood like a monument. Some yards away Quimby was assembling his meat safe on a bench set up in front of his shelter on the shore. Steven gauged him. The man was no taller than he, but a good deal thicker in the body. His blows would have beef behind them. This was an added reason for persuading him peaceably.

Quimby looked at him from beneath heavy brows when he went forward. Steven said nothing. Walking slowly and keeping his manner casual, he sat on a palm log near the work bench. He gave no greeting.

After a moment of regarding him suspiciously, Quimby said, "You come to get lard you got another guess. Unless you want to buy. I ain't holding up the price any."

"I didn't come to buy," Steven told him.

"What did you come for, then?" Quimby asked.

"For the whole hog, free," Steven answered.

Quimby snorted. He took up squares of evenly cut cypress boards measuring several feet across and began to fit them together. He started to nail, taking great care in making a box of the boards.

Steven let him work for a time. Then he said, "I reckon you don't know so good how things is run around here. For one thing, there's supposed to be a deputy sheriff. But nobody will take the job. We figure if there was a law officer he might get so nosy as to make opposition to him and start wrongdoing. We're kind of proud of ourselves for all working like one to make this a law-abiding place."

"I ain't committed any crime," Quimby stated.

"Nor I ain't saying you have," Steven told him. "I'm just trying to point out what it's supposed to be like here. It's the same with things found on the beach. We figure that's what Providence sends, so it's share and share alike no matter who finds them. And especial when it's something everybody needs, like shortening is needed now."

Quimby kept on nailing when he replied, "They already told me that."

"It ain't neighborly to keep it to yourself," Steven instructed.

"I found it. It's mine. I offered to sell," Quimby defended himself. "Even to Bethune, so he could make a profit."

Steven shook his head. "He won't buy. And neither will anybody else. Anybody who did would be an outcast—same as whoever took the deputy job. Like you'll be if you keep on."

"I don't care about that," Quimby stated. "And I don't believe they'll go without. They'll come buying nights when nobody sees them."

Steven glanced at the barrel. "You can wait and find out while it goes rancid on you. And you can learn something else."

Quimby stopped his work long enough to run a huge hand through his bleached hair and ask, "What d'you mean?"

"When other things is washed up, lots, that takes everybody to gather them, they're shipped out and the profits divided. You won't be counted part of that."

"I don't see where there's enough to find to let that worry me," Quimby answered confidently.

"Every couple of years there's a whole shipload. The things needed is distributed. The rest goes out. Once, but one thing in a load was a case of lace from Europe. You still see it on women's dresses, but most of it brought more than what twenty of your barrels would fetch."

"I got the lard right now," Quimby pointed out.

"Most everything around here is wrecked goods," Steven continued, "shared by all. Even the cats. Another time a hundred gross of razors come up on the beach. Maybe you got an idea of what they was worth."

"Not much chance of that happening again," Quimby said skeptically.

"That's right," Steven agreed, "and there ain't much chance of sometime a chest of gold bullion being rolled up on the beach. Except that some of it's known to be lost out there and them waves can handle just about anything when they're of a mind to. Of course you might find such a thing by yourself and keep it like you're doing the lard. Then again somebody else might come on it and you wouldn't be counted a share. You got to weigh your chances on a thing like that."

Steven saw that this time Quimby was impressed. But he wasn't convinced. In making a lightning calculation of his chances, he seemed to figure that his luck alone would suffice. But he was thinking it over. "That ain't the way we do things up to Titusville," he said.

"This ain't Titusville," Steven pointed out.

Quimby had finished the meat safe. Now he contemplated the wooden box he had created. He took a stingaree tail from the work bench and began to pick his teeth with it thoughtfully.

The mention of the gold bullion was between them more than the meat safe when Steven got up to look at the box. He picked it up and held it to the light and said, "Looks tight enough." He tried the lid which fastened down evenly and securely.

"That there," Quimby said proudly, "will keep my meat just like I had ice."

Steven glanced at him. "It won't unless you know the rest of it."

Quimby looked startled.

Steven told him, "Dead air like you'll have in here will spoil meat faster than being left in the open."

"How else does it work?" Quimby demanded.

"You got a fire going in your stove?" At Quimby's nod, Steven instructed, "Get a couple of live coals."

Wondering, Quimby went into his shack. Steven stooped and gathered a handful of white sand. This he deposited in a corner of the bottom of the meat safe. When Quimby returned with a few glowing coals carried on his stove shovel, Steven directed him to put them on the sand in the box.

Then Steven took out the sulphur. He sprinkled a little of it on the coals. Strong fumes rose as he shut the box. "That way your meat will keep for a week or more," he told Quimby. "There won't be any sulphur taste."

In silence Quimby received the remainder of the sulphur. It was only after a moment that he asked, "You're giving me this?"

"To show you how we share what we know here, too," Steven told him. "I'm glad to do it."

A peculiar look came on Quimby's face. Steven decided there wouldn't be any fight. He welcomed that, for he still couldn't work up much emotion about battling Quimby.

Then he thought he was wrong. Quimby's glance caught his barrel of lard. He scowled. He made a movement of flinging the packet of sulphur on the table. But the movement was arrested. Instead, Quimby looked sheepish. He gave a short laugh and said, "I guess you saved me from making a fool of myself over the safe."

"Everybody's got to learn it for the first time," Steven told him.

Quimby looked away, across the lake. Without glancing at Steven, he murmured, "It near about broke my back getting that lard here. Maybe the two of us can handle it easier." He ended on a question. "If it's to be handed out at the store?"

Steven answered softly. "That's the usual way we do it."

This had no more than been decided when there came a rustling at one side of Quimby's shack. Cap Jim, followed by a lurching Durgan and half a dozen men, came out.

Steven began, "I told you—"

"You did it!" Cap Jim boomed. He thumped Steven on the back. He took a surprised Quimby's hand and pumped it, telling him, "You got more sense than I figured."

"I thought I was going to see a fight," one of the men complained.

Quimby turned on Steven. "You meant to fight me?"

"That was the only other way."

"I would have obliged you," Quimby said. He shook his head at the customs here. "But now there's no need."

In the bushes, at the other side of the shack, Steven saw the little white face of the boy, Adie. He didn't come out, but thought he was hidden and couldn't be seen. He looked scared. Then he darted back, disappearing.

Three

QUIMBY, WHEN HE UNDERSTOOD that he wasn't held in contempt, showed signs of his previous attitude not being his real nature, but a front he put up to the world. He helped to carry the lard barrel to the store. He managed a laugh at Durgan who bemoaned his promise to sign the temperance petition.

Steven was glad the affair with Quimby had come out as it had. He would have fought the man, but feeling the way he did was no manner in which to go into a fight. Right now he was more concerned with something else, with the actions of the strange boy.

He didn't see Adie on the way back. Once there, Steven went immediately to the rear of the store building. At the door of Cap Jim's room he stopped. He listened. He heard deep breathing. That made him wonder the more.

He went out at the rear, thinking it over. He ran a hand through his hair. He felt how tousled it was. He took a comb hanging from the wall on the end of a cord and looking into a mirror placed near it, he drew the comb through his hair. In the glass the tanned contour of his face was long, not handsome, but pleasantly molded, the mouth liberal, the skin clean. He gave his mustache a few swipes before he dropped the comb and went back inside with resolve.

He eased the door open. Adie lay on the bed. His eyes were closed. He seemed to be asleep, but something told Steven that he wasn't. The boy was behaving in curious fashion. Why had he kept to his room, sneaked out to Quimby's, and then hurried back to pretend he had been asleep here all the time?

Steven had the impulse to speak to him, to question him again. But Adie looked so innocent and harmless lying there that he restrained himself. There would be time for that.

Quietly, he closed the door.

In the store the men were obtaining a supply of lard to take to their wives. They were wrapping it in heavy paper and Quimby, grinning self-consciously, was ladling it out with a huge wooden spoon Doc had provided. The Deacon had rushed home to get a lard pail. As Quimby filled this, Doc, leaning against the counter, exclaimed, "Listen to this here!"

The men turned to him. In his hands Doc held a letter which he now waved indignantly. He announced:

"It's from the government, right from the head post office. And it says we can't have the name of Palm City because there's a Palm City already in the state. It says on account of this the mails are getting mixed up, and will get mixed up more. It tells us—anyway, it suggests—we get another name."

A man said, "Well, Jiminy Christ!"

The Deacon cleared his throat with disapproval of this remark.

"What are we going to do about it?" Doc demanded.

"We're going to fix ourselves another name," Cap Jim replied. "You can't go against the government."

"What's it going to be?" demanded Durgan. His voice was thick.

They thought. Steven slid on top of the counter to sit there, dangling his legs.

"How about going back to 'Lake Worth'?" asked a man.

"We changed that because people thought it meant the lake and didn't know there was anything else here."

" 'Palmville,' " another suggested.

"Too many villes already," was the objection to this. "Besides, there's no distinction to that."

" 'Pineapple.' "

"They'd laugh at that."

They considered some more. But no one had a further idea. "Perhaps," said the Deacon, "we had better have a meeting of all the settlers and pick one that way, by vote."

"This town's got to be named right away," Doc objected. "The government says we have to decide quick. Who's got a name?"

Steven, looking out the window at palm fronds brushing against each other in the wind, pictured his swinging feet moving along the beach. "Maybe," he suggested, "something like 'Palm Beach' would do."

There was silence.

"That ain't bad," one man observed.

"Not bad at all," said another.

"It fits," a third agreed.

"Hell," said Cap Jim, "it's good."

"It's damned good," Durgan muttered.

Doc said, "Looks like you give it, Stevie." His eyes filled with sudden moisture. "You come here a orphan boy and now you named the town."

To Steven's confusion, the Deacon came over to him and wrung his hand. The Deacon's hand was clammy.

The men began to file out, the new name of the town on their lips. Steven dropped from the counter. He took up a small empty can and walked over to Quimby, telling him, "I want to carry some to the Pagets." He said nothing to anybody in the store about Adie, that he meant to ask Jesse Paget's opinion about the boy.

Steven walked down the path leading to the Thomas House, south from the store. Before reaching it, he turned off on a narrower path, going a short way toward the ocean. Here the Pagets had come to live only a week ago. Before that they lived in one of the three houses composing the settlement of Jupiter at the foot of the lighthouse there. From the light Jesse had carried the mail the eighty-four miles to Miami. Each way took him four days, eight in all, leaving him almost no time at home. Now that Steven was taking over the greater part of the route, the Pagets had moved down.

Their cabbage house occupied a small clearing. In front of it stood a pump with its handle off. When Steven strode up he could hear Jesse inside speaking excitedly while a full laughing girl's voice answered him. From the open porch, outside, another voice addressed Steven, saying, "Never seed sich goin's on. Givin' up the best part of good work so he kin be with his woman every minute of the day. An' night."

Steven stepped up on the porch, under the eave of the thick palmetto thatch, and said, "Howdy, Missus Paget."

Linda Paget, lean to stringiness, clad in a shapeless dress, sat in her shoofly chair. One foot, placed on a pedal, activated a rod that went up straight in back of her. From this there extended an arm to which was attached strands of soft cotton fringe. As she pressed the pedal with her foot, the fringe was waved back and forth at her head. And though the wind today had driven away mosquitoes and sandflies, Linda pedaled just the same, out of habit.

The bright clear eyes of the Cracker woman regarded Steven accusingly. "An' you're the one takin' my son's bread an' butter right out of his mouth."

"Jesse hasn't wanted to walk the mail all the way from Jupiter to Miami ever since he got married." Steven didn't try to cajole the old lady. She could beat him every time.

"Who knows that better'n me?" she demanded. She didn't mind the fringe when it brushed smartly over her face as she pedaled harder. She didn't even blink. She looked at the can in his hand. "What you got there?"

Steven told her. The seamed face nodded approval and she said, "That's the way to do, rightly. Keep up the old neighborly manners. Glad to see it. Don't know what most young folks is comin' to these days, what with their frippery way of doin' things. Like Jesse now."

The door opened. Jesse asked, "Talking about us, Ma?'

Jesse had his arm around a girl whose figure was solid with shapeliness. Her fine firm breasts pushed straight out, tightening the apron that nearly covered her dress. The dark beauty of her face was accentuated by blue-black hair that fell to her shoulders. Red lips were held back from flashing white teeth. "She's got a husband now instead of a visitor," Jesse announced.

"I don't know what I'll do with him all the time," Della told Steven. "He'll wear me out."

Jesse roared, elaborating her reference, "Wear *you* out? I guess I know who'll be wore out!"

They laughed, clinging to each other.

"That ain't no way to talk," Linda said. "Right before Steven."

"It's all right for you to do it," Jesse taunted his mother. "You're jealous, Grandma."

"Don't you call me Gran'ma!" The shoofly chair worked furiously. "You ain't done a thing yit to call me like that."

"We got a good start," Jesse asserted.

The chair stopped operating for a moment. "You mean to say—?" Linda looked at her daughter-in-law. Her expression was accusing, bitter at what Linda could do for her son, at how the wife could take him away from the mother.

Steven, with a horrible fascination at this talk, felt his own eyes drawn to the body of the girl.

Della's big eyes flashed. "Jesse's carrying on. He's way past himself. It's the Cracker part of him," she told Linda, "that comes from you making him do it."

"Never you mind about that!"

"Well," said Jesse, "it ain't because we ain't tried—when we had the chance."

"It ain't nice," said Linda. "With Steven bein' female-shy like he is."

The three of them regarded Steven. He said nothing. He was appalled and confused. The mere marriage of his friend had seemed to divide them. This talk drove Jesse entirely away from him, made him a stranger who occupied another and fearsome world.

Genially, Jesse said of him, "He's got to get over having his tongue tied up in knots every time a man and a woman is mentioned. It ain't natural."

Della told her husband, "You get at fixing that pump handle or we won't have any water for the morning."

Steven's gratitude was silent, but plain, when his eyes met those of Della for an instant.

"We'll talk some while I fix the pump," Jesse said. He moved off the porch and Steven made to follow him.

"He's comin' in with us," Linda declared. "We got to have somebody different to talk to once."

Jesse waved a hand and went off to the pump. Steven followed the two women inside the house, where he gave Della the lard.

Mosquito netting covered the window openings. The walls and floor were made of timbers from the hulls of ships. Some were curved and here and there the head of a copper bolt gleamed. Through wide clinks, and above the slats of the high-pointed ceiling, there appeared the inner side of the cabbage thatch, the palm fans bleached, dry and crisp.

Della busied herself at the glowing stove while Linda began to set the sawed-plank table in the middle of the room. Steven took to one of the unwieldy chairs placed about it. "Know where my table's always set fer one more, don't you?" the old lady cackled.

"Maybe," said Steven, "I oughtn't to be so presuming, even though you hang out the longest latchstring of anybody along the coast. I ain't been asked yet."

"A hongry mouth is always welcome here," Linda lectured him, "as long as we got somethin' to put in it." She stopped placing tin plates on the table to point to a rattlesnake skin nailed over the planks on one wall. It was fully twelve feet long and so wide that it extended across several of the timbers. "You see that there skin?"

"It's mighty," Steven said politely.

Della turned from the stove and addressed the old lady. "You told Steven about it twice already. And he must have heard it a dozen times before I married you along with Jesse."

"You shet yore sass," Linda told her.

Della stirred noisily in a pot.

"The thing that was in that there skin," Linda related to Steven, "up an' bit my man an' kilt him. An' after it did so, I kilt it. I shot it as dead as Jesse's pa."

Linda's voice quavered on a proud note. She gazed at the skin. "That's what come of me marryin' to a Cuban. He didn't know no better than to git hisself rattler-bit. An' that's why I give up his name an' took back to my own. Nobody who didn't live as him ain't got any right fer me to carry his name."

Steven nodded. He understood why the old lady insisted upon being known as Paget. It was less of a reminder.

A clanking sound came from the pump where Jesse worked. Linda busied herself again, keeping up her chatter. "An' now Jesse goes down to Key West an' gits another Cuban in the family. Mebbe she was born an' went to school there, but she's a Cuban jist the same."

Iron banged at the stove, matching the noise Jesse was making outside. Steven, uncomfortable, searched for a way to stop the old lady.

"The same blood findin' out its kind," she went on. "Iffen it keeps on like it looks it's goin' to from what they give out, there won't be no good blood left. Mostly," Linda said scornfully, "it'll be Cuban."

Della, holding a hot dish with her apron, brought it to the table. "That's better than what Crackers got in them. Crackers," she explained to Steven, "got some kind of thin soup for blood, giving them no flesh on their bones." She stood straight and blooming, her vigor in startling contrast with the skinny old lady.

As if recognizing her defeat, and knowing that she could fight back only with spirit, Linda cried, "No good comes of mixing Cracker an' Cuban, you mark my word!"

Steven couldn't stand the fight any more. In desperation he raised his voice to make himself heard. "I see I better get me some kind of protection from the wildcats when I come here."

Della subsided and returned to her stove. Linda, cackling and muttering, went about the rest of her own work.

The remainder of the meal was put on the table. "Set by," Linda said. "You out there, Jesse! Set by!"

Jesse didn't reply or appear.

"Call yore dog," Linda said to Della. "He only comes fer you now."

With an angry glance at the old woman, Della cried, "Jesse! Come on to supper!"

The pump could be heard working. It stopped, and Jesse came in. He sat with them at the table. Heads went down reverently for the grace.

Jesse, cocking an eye at Della, pronounced it. "Grits is ready," he intoned, "and grits is tough, and, thank God, I had grits enough."

Della giggled. Steven grinned. Linda catechized, "That's what it's like havin' a foreigner for a son, to say the Lord's word."

They ate grits, yams, snapper steaks, and sour orange biscuits. Linda and Della were mostly silent, nursing their spat. Jesse speared at the food, his fat little stomach pushed against the edge of the table. Steven asked, "What's the news upcountry?"

Jesse chewed on a big mouthful, swallowed before it was ready, and gulped, "I collected more than enough to make it worth dividing."

"The government ain't actually getting at building the houses of refuge on the beach?" Steven inquired.

"They're supposed to start the first one any day now," Jesse said. "I know we heard that before, but this time it looks like fact. Anyway, I got in my application for the keeper's job. It don't look like we'll be living here long, but going down the line. Then my two womenfolk can have all the room they want to do their fighting."

He glanced at Della. She had a sullen look on her face, and didn't respond. Linda snorted.

"That ain't all the news," Jesse went on. "Not by a long sight. There's no chance of the regular railroad being built down below Titusville for years, but they're thinking of putting in a narrow-gauge eight miles from Jupiter to the head of the lake."

"What's the good of that?" Steven wanted to know.

"It'll be part of better service for goods, passengers, and the mail," Jesse revealed. "They'll put in a steamer instead of the sailboat on the Indian River. Then from this end of the narrow-gauge there'll be a naphtha launch to here on the lake."

Steven contemplated this, impressed. "Why," he said, "that'll be practically express service."

Jesse pointed with his iron fork and warned, "Pretty soon this country will be so populated it won't be worth living in. It's already so you don't have elbow room any more."

"I can't see where it's so crowded," Steven observed. "About a hundred people hereabouts, and not more than that in the whole north tip of the county."

"I want to be where you ain't living in somebody's lap all the time," Jesse declared.

After the meal, Linda went stiffly to her chamber. Della worked at the dishes while the two men talked at the table. It began to get dark outside, the night falling quickly. Steven began to tell Jesse about Adie when suddenly he was shocked to hear Della crying. Jesse jumped up and went to her. In the brief twilight he tried to soothe her sobs. Steven heard from Della, "I don't know why I ever came up to this wilderness. . . . Living with that old woman!"

Steven left his chair and went outside. He sat on the step. From inside, he could still hear their voices. Gradually, Della's sobbing came to a stop. Jesse was whispering. In a little while Della gave a low laugh. In suppressed tones, she protested and laughed at the same time. There came the sound of a kiss, then another. A lamp was lighted inside, throwing its dull yellow glow through the mosquito netting.

Jesse came out, to sit by Steven on the step. He sighed happily. "You got to know how to deal with women. But I guess I couldn't ever do without one after this."

Steven didn't reply. Most of his embarrassment left him. Again he told Jesse about Adie and the boy's mysterious behavior. "What do you think about me taking him?" he asked.

Jesse considered. "I took along some pretty queer folks when I was doing it. You saw some of them when you came with me. I don't know about this boy. I don't see much he could do to you, unless like Doc said he happens to be in with the combers. Maybe they'll try something some day, maybe they won't." Jesse glanced over his shoulder as if he could see Della through the wall. "I expect it's a thing you got to decide for yourself now."

Four

STEVEN WAS UP AT DAWN. He prepared coffee, biscuits, and grits in the store kitchen. The mail bag was already packed in his white oilcloth haversack. He went to knock on Adie's door. The boy answered sleepily and, in a few minutes, came out. His cap was on; he was ready to go.

Adie sat with him before the food. The boy ate ravenously. Steven observed, "Doc told me you wouldn't come out for supper last night."

The boy looked wary, but replied easily, "I wasn't hungry. And I wasn't feeling so good after the boat trip."

Steven couldn't blame him there. But he pointed out, "You went to Quimby's yesterday."

Adie's gray eyes gleamed. "I heard the talking about it in the store. I always like to see a fight. I'll bet you could have licked him."

Steven didn't let the flattery work on him. "You didn't show yourself," he said. "You acted like you was sneaking there and back."

Adie looked hurt. "That's because I heard you saying nobody was to go. I thought maybe you wouldn't want me there."

The boy was ready with his explanations. And they sounded plausible. Steven thought they were almost too plausible. He sensed some unknown quality about the boy. But he couldn't quite place his finger on it. He was about to ask Adie why he pretended to be asleep when he wasn't and just then his searching gaze caught the eyes of the boy directly.

Adie stared at him with the same appeal he had yesterday. Fright that Steven might not take him after all shone through welling tears. He dropped his long lashes and looked down at his food, not touching it.

"Go on and finish eating," Steven told him. "I'm going to trust you, but don't you forget that."

Steven rose and slung his haversack to his back. He hitched at the canvas straps over his shoulders to set them right. Adie joined him. As they went out, Doc called from his room, "Look out for them combers now, Stevie."

"I'll see you Saturday," Steven assured him.

At the beach the sun was behind a bank of clouds from which the dying northeaster blew. Steven glanced up and down. There was nothing of consequence washed ashore. He looked with approval at Adie's bare feet and then stooped to remove his shoes, warning the boy of the trip ahead, "It's sixty-six miles."

Adie stood as if uncertain, gazing one moment down the beach and the next at Steven. But he said resolutely, "I'm a good walker."

Steven tied the laces of his shoes together and slung them over his shoulder. "It takes three days."

Adie looked surprised. His lips moved one over the other. Obviously, he hadn't expected it to take so long. "Where do we sleep?" he asked.

"On the beach." Steven rolled his trousers high up on his thighs; his legs were deeply tanned, looking like long stockings.

Adie pulled his cap tighter on his head to prevent the wind from carrying it away. "I haven't brought anything to eat." He eyed Steven's haversack. "You don't look as if you've got much."

"We find most of it. It ain't hard to get as much as you can do anything with. You go first. I'll tell you how to walk so as to make it the easiest."

His clothes pressed flat against the left side of his small figure by the wind, Adie started out. They kept to the edge of the water, where the sand was hardest. Steven watched the boy's moving legs. He walked with short steps, but freely, his feet leaving delicate impressions in the sand. He didn't seem to mind when the water occasionally washed up over his ankles.

Steven instructed the boy in his own peculiar gait. The slanting beach made the distance lower to put down one foot than the other, and the walking took this into account, so that there was no tiring from the difference. The trick was to be just a little quicker with the right foot going south, and quicker with the left foot going north. Jesse had taught him that, proclaiming him a true beach walkist when he accomplished it.

Adie caught on quickly, and soon he was walking more off the toes of his right foot than off the heel.

Steven was happy. He had longed for the beach to be his own, and now it was. He exulted in his long stride covering it. He recognized pieces of debris as if they were old friends. He breathed deeply of the faint salt odor of the sea. The sun lifted itself above the clouds, warming him, lighting the world starkly. He asked Adie, "You see the fish?"

Adie looked far out, to where the Gulf Stream, bucking the wind, could be seen raising itself with jagged chops against the horizon.

"In the breakers," Steven told him, "while they're still green, before they fall."

Adie searched again, and at first couldn't see them. Then he did, and cried out with pleasure at the sight of the silvery flashes held for an instant as though jellied in the lifting water. Adie stopped to look until Steven said, "We keep on, with me telling when to rest. Unless you get tuckered."

The boy didn't tire, or at least he didn't say so or give any evidence of it. As they proceeded, he seemed to become more at ease. He exclaimed at shells, and stooped as he walked to pick them up, stuffing his pockets with bleeding teeth, cat's-paws, turkey-wings, and pieces of coral. He found a fragile paper nautilus intact, and carried it in one hand so that it would not be broken. He snatched up a brown sea heart and Steven told him he could polish it for a watch-fob.

When he discovered a sand dollar Steven took it from him and without warning broke the brittle white disk in two. Catching what fell out, he exhibited to Adie five tiny white birdlike shapes. They were so perfect that they seemed ready to fly. The boy took them appreciatively, but at the same time he looked gloomy at the destruction of his sand dollar. Steven said, "You'll come across all you want."

Steven didn't question him further. The boy would talk about himself if he cared to. Steven expected him to before the trip was long under way, but instead of drawing it out he wanted it to come of its own accord. That there was something for him to tell, even that there was something Steven must be on guard against, he was now sure.

At mid-morning they left the beach and Steven led the way across a low sand ridge until he and Adie stood on the edge of inner water. At their feet lay an old skiff. Across the quarter of a mile of water a long island lay in the narrow end of Lake Worth. "That's Hypoluxo," Steven told Adie. "In Indian it means 'Round Mound.'"

As Steven stepped to the skiff and prepared to board it, Adie hung back and asked, "This ain't the regular way?"

"The island's mine," Steven answered. "I look at it most times I go by. And we got to get some of the best potatoes there is, to take along."

Adie hesitated. They eyed each other. Steven didn't understand the boy's reluctance. He was about to speak, to ask sharp questions, when Adie climbed in the boat with him.

Steven sculled across, disturbing a flock of pelicans from whose roosts, in the sea plums, a lacy curtain of white droppings hung against the green. From absurd awkwardness on their perches the great birds took on a grace in tandem flight, gliding against the sky. They began to fish, one by one folding their wings, and plummeting head-first into the water, to disappear, and then come to the surface again working their cavernous beaks over a catch.

Adie watched, fascinated. The boy was silent when Steven grounded the boat on the shore. Under, up, and over the thick vegetation grew myriads of morning glories. They appeared to cover everything with their purple and pink, giving the impression that they blanketed the island for its mile of length and several hundred yards of width.

Once more Adie exclaimed at something new and attractive to him. He picked one of the flowers and carried it by the stem in his fist. Steven told him, "This is morning-glory land. You see them like this and you know it's the best land for growing."

He knelt and began to dig at the roots of what looked something like morning-glory plants, except that the leaves were larger and there were no blossoms on them. He turned over the rich, powdery brown loam. Four tremendous sweet potatoes came into his hand. "Put them in my sack," he instructed Adie, "and you'll taste something you never had that good before."

Adie slipped the potatoes under the flap of the sack. Steven stood up and led the boy through a grove of scraggy trees. In a persimmon a possum hung head down placidly eating a green fruit held in its tiny forepaws. Adie yelped with delight, but the animal paid no attention, going on with its meal.

"He'll get a bellyache doing that," Steven prophesied.

Adie watched the possum over his shoulder as they went on to trees bearing large yellow and orange fruit whose surface was covered with knobs. Adie reached, saying, "I never picked an orange from a tree before." He gazed at the rough skin of the fruit, opened his mouth as if to remark on its unusual appearance, then began to peel it.

"We'll look at the house," Steven said.

A low, thatched, driftwood structure stood under an overbranching wall of pines. Fastened to each of its gables was a pair of deer antlers. Up the walls and over these grew the morning glories, rampant in their possession. Steven brushed the plants out of the way at the steps leading to the smooth glistening mahogany door of the house. Tapping it, Steven explained, "It came from a wrecked ship's cabin."

He creaked the door open and they went in.

The sizable single room had little furniture in it, yet didn't seem bare, but warm and lived-in. There were two chairs made from knocking out the end of a barrel, sawing a quarter of it away and fastening the end for a seat in the middle. A wide wooden bunk had thick strands of hempen rope woven for combined slats and mattress. A weathered sea chest stood in a corner, and in another was a cast-iron stove. In the coquina rock of the fireplace the spirals of shells could be seen. Two bearskins on the floor were cleanly black. Across them lay bars of sunlight which entered through chinks in the shutters closed over the paneless windows.

Steven sat in one of the barrel chairs. It was always like another home to him here; he came sometimes to stay for days, and he liked the moment now. He listened to the wind stirring the crisp palmetto walls.

Adie took to the other barrel, his slight figure lost in its capaciousness. The boy stared about with round eyes. His admiration was frank when he said:

"It's like Robinson Crusoe's house. You say it's yours? You can really live here?" While still staring, he began to suck at his peeled fruit. His mouth puckered and a wry expression wrinkled his face.

"That's a wild orange you got there. The tree's only waiting to be budded with sweet. That's one of the things I aim to do here some day."

Adie sucked tentatively at the huge orange as Steven explained how the island of Hypoluxo was his. A man called Uncle Charlie, a Yankee living in Tallahassee, had escaped Confederate conscription by coming here to settle. Uncle Charlie had homesteaded the island and been fond of Steven as a boy. When he left, some years ago, he had given the island and his house to Steven.

"Did he give you a paper, or something to prove it?" Adie inquired.

"Everybody knows it," Steven replied. "That's enough."

Adie shook his head, gazing worriedly at Steven, concerned that Steven might not be able to prove his ownership of such a desirable place. He spoke surprisingly. "Is this where you'll come when you get married?"

Steven wasn't disturbed by the boy's question. It didn't seem to trouble him that Adie asked it. There wasn't the same knowing, rather superior, mocking quality in his interest as there was in that of other people. It was more innocent.

He welcomed the invitation to talk. He was astonished to

realize that he wanted to talk about it. Mostly he had sat here and thought and dreamed by himself.

"Yes, sir," he said. "I'll carry her right up those steps and through that door. This place never had a woman, and that's what it needs. It ain't so bad for a woman, either, if she's the kind maybe I'll find. There's flowers for her to look at and a whole island to call her own. And you don't locate morning-glory land like this all the time. I'm hoping to find one who'll plant herself here and grow and bloom just like they do. And who'll like the birds and other living things. Even the snakes when they can be friendly-like, such as a big old black snake who comes around the house eating palmetto bugs and lizards and scorpions and keeping away the rattlers and moccasins. You hear the birds? It's them I'm wanting her to like most."

They listened. There was the shrill call of a parakeet. A limpkin wailed insanely. Ground doves cooed sensuously, almost indecently. A woodpecker tapped. A chuck-will's-widow whistled and another answered. Most of all there was the continuous message of a mockingbird, scolding between imitations of the other calls.

"That mocker can make you believe he's about anything," Steven said. "You like them?"

Adie didn't answer. He was looking at Steven as though he had been told a wonderful story which enthralled him so much that he was still living it.

The stare of the boy made Steven conscious of what he had said, of how he had lost himself in speaking as he never had before to another human being. He said shortly, "We'll get back and on."

They left the house and walked, shin-deep, through the morning glories again. Standing among them, high on long-stemmed scarlet legs, was a small flock of large, brilliantly pink birds. Their necks arched up for nearly a yard, to end in a head with a vivid orange and black beak. The flamingoes rose as one, and flapped silently away.

Before Adie could exclaim at this, he saw something else. A hump-backed creature lumbered along the ground, its dry gray shell appearing and disappearing among the flowers.

"Gopher," announced Steven. "Uncle Charlie brought some here and raised them for meat. We'll let this one stay, not wanting to be burdened down with too much to carry."

"A gopher's something like a squirrel," Adie protested as they reached the boat, "except it lives in a hole in the ground. That was a turtle, the biggest I ever saw."

Sculling back to the ocean ridge, Steven replied, "I'll tell you why it wasn't, and why it can't get away from the island. This is the story:

"God made the turtle and when the Devil saw it the Devil said that was an easy thing to make. God told him that nobody except Him could create, and if the Devil thought he could make a turtle he could go ahead and try. The Devil made one, and then each threw his turtle into the water. God's turtle swam around and had a good time, while the Devil's turtle couldn't swim at all. It crawled out of the water to land, where it dug a hole and lived. The Devil was pretty disappointed and said, 'Mine may not be a turtle, but it'll go for one.' So after that it was called a gopher."

Adie giggled. His noise was girlish. Steven noted that in his speech, and sometimes in the manner of his movements, the boy showed signs of being almost feminine. Steven supposed that young boys, not yet having developed the characteristics of a man, were like that.

Adie twisted the morning glory he still carried, threw away the pulp of the orange which he had finished, and picked up his paper nautilus from where he had left it on a thwart. He gazed at Hypoluxo, back at Steven, and then at Hypoluxo again as if living there would be the best thing in the world.

During the morning the wind eased to a steady breeze and the sea began to lose its riotousness, aided by the dropping of the tide. Shortly before noon they came to an outcropping of rough gray rock which extended into the water. On the dry beach plain above this Steven let down his pack and told Adie, "For mid meal I'll show you something."

He took the boy to the rock, on which they both stepped gingerly to avoid the sharp points. Embedded in it, and sometimes throwing itself half out as if writhing in agony, was a tremendous rusted anchor chain. Steven explained that hundreds of years ago a ship had been wrecked here. Coquina rock had been deposited to form over its skeleton, and all that showed now was the chain.

Adie touched the encrusted iron with an exploring toe. Steven, for the first time in his life, felt fatherly. It was a queer, warming feeling that made him want to instruct Adie further.

In the rock were deep pot-holes, washed by the rollers, in which swarms of small pan-fish milled. "You ever catch fish with your bare hands?" Steven asked.

Adie put his hands in back of him and said, "You can't do it."

"Watch," said Steven. He went a few yards to shallow pools worn in the rock. More fish were here, trapped when left by the receding tide. Steven bent down and put his hands in the water. It was tepid, almost hot, from the sun. He grabbed, missed, grabbed again, and brought out a wriggling sailor's choice. "They ain't hard to get," he said. "The heat has dulled them."

Adie held back until Steven captured two more. Then the boy knelt at another pool. His first efforts were half-hearted, as though he didn't like it. He caught one fish, laughed as if being tickled, and lost it when it slipped between his fingers. He got another, which he added to Steven's flopping pile. In a moment the boy was enjoying himself hugely, getting the fish as fast as Steven.

When they had several dozen, Steven told him, "I'll dress some of them. You hunt up wood and build a fire. Matches are in my sack."

Adie stood hesitantly for a moment and then went up the beach alone. Steven took a claspknife from a pocket and opened its blade. He gutted all the fish. Swiftly, he scaled half of them. Washing these in a pool where their brothers still swam, he laid them on the ocean rock and deftly filleted them. As he strode to the beach, gulls swooped down to get at the remains.

Steven nodded approval of the brisk fire Adie had going. He put the prepared fish on the open flap of his haversack and stuffed the others inside. "Folks complain that the mail stinks some," he explained, "but I don't see where it hurts them or the letters any." He took out a small fry-pan, a coffee-boil consisting of a lard can, and two tin cups.

Carrying the can and cups, Steven led Adie to the thick brush above the beach. They entered this, striding through tall switch grass and edging carefully around cacti. They began to descend from the slight elevation until they came to a place where the earth was mixed sand and marl and where palmetto grew.

The heads of several trees had been torn out, the delicate, tasty bud removed. The work was roughly done, as though by claws. At the sight of it Steven searched about near by on the ground. He found several holes where again claw marks were to be seen. They were less than a foot deep, but clear water shone in one of them. "Nothing like having bears do your work for you," he said.

"Bears did that?" asked Adie. He sounded frightened and he shrank back, looking about in the undergrowth.

"That's the way they get water here to drink. It's the way we get it, too." Steven dipped the tin cups and handed one to Adie. The boy didn't drink until after Steven. The water was fresh and fairly cool. Steven half-filled the coffee-boil. He handed this to Adie while he cut two green palm fans.

When they returned to the beach, Steven let out a yell that made Adie jump to one side in fright until he saw what caused it. A blue heron stood with its grave stance near the haversack and was snatching at it. Steven yelled again and picked up a heavy piece of broken shell. He threw it at the heron. It landed to startle the bird, and instantly it took off, carrying a piece of fish in its bill.

"He only got one," Steven said when he and Adie reached the sack. "I'll go short."

"I can't eat six," Adie told him. The boy seemed torn between delight at the things he was seeing and the thought of the bears, for he glanced once or twice at the scrub. He looked as if he regretted coming along with the mail carrier.

Steven told him there was no harm to be expected from the animals on the beach. They came to it only to search out turtle eggs, a delicacy which they would work themselves to skin and bone to find. There were no eggs now, the turtles laying only in summer; but with the eternal summer here the bears sometimes got their seasons mixed.

As he drew things from his sack, Steven was reasonably sure that Adie had never been along the beach before. But then people could act and pretend, even a round-eyed boy. He brought out hard biscuits from the sack while the fish fried to a brown crisp, and then served both on the palm fans. He poured the coffee and watched the boy carefully when Adie asked, "What did Mister Bethune mean about the beachcombers?"

Five

STEVEN EXPLAINED that three renegades, wanted men and generally reckless individuals, lived back of the beach farther down where they would pass tomorrow. It was generally understood that the men had women with them, girls, but no one had ever seen these. The men preyed on ships wrecked in storms. When there weren't any wrecks they hunted plume birds. Sometimes they went up to the lake or down to Miami.

Adie listened with intense interest. "You mean murderers?" he asked.

One of them, Steven admitted, was supposed to be. His name was Theron. He had been here a long time. Originally he came from Georgia, where he was said to have killed a man. Years ago Theron had set up an empire of fellow outlaws back of the beach. He put the Negro fugitives to work. When they wanted a share of the profits—so the story about him went— he gave them a bullet instead. People all along the coast were afraid of him, even the law officers. One ambitious sheriff who went to arrest Theron had been forced to work for a month before being sent back to Miami.

Adie's eyes widened as he gazed down the beach. "Where do they find the women?" he asked.

"Where they can," Steven said. "If they got them at all."

Adie looked at Steven's broad arms and stated, "I guess you can handle them if they give trouble."

"The telling of that," Steven said, "would be in the doing." He knew the beachcombers for being no fighters. He and Jesse had talked with them a number of times. He never seriously expected any difficulty from them, though he suspected the mail must be a temptation to them. The realization came to him that now he carried it alone.

Adie looked sure, then doubtful, as if he had a fear not only for himself but for Steven as well. Steven saw no indication that the boy was acquainted in any way with the combers. That, he felt certain, was not the unknown thing behind Adie. Still he couldn't place his finger on anything it might be. And the more baffled he became the more warily he watched.

Adie's sense of danger seemed to leave him as they walked through the afternoon. He delighted in striding on the soft **green** sea moss that covered flat rocks they came to in stretches

Here they saw an octopus shrunken back into a crevice. "I get pretty low down before I eat them," Steven told him.

The boy chased crabs caught out of their holes, but never captured one. He clamored with interest when, late in the afternoon, they came to the fore part of a wreck slanted and half-buried in the sand. The timbers, bleached white as a bone, Steven explained were too far away from any settlement to make it worth while to transport them. The copper sheathing of the hull had been stripped away; it brought fifteen cents a pound and was as good as money. Only one glory remained.

At the prow, set under the shattered bowsprit, there was the figurehead of a naked woman. Shapely and fully rounded, she was painted an alabaster white. Her paint still stood against the attack of the sun. The spots where she had chipped were in peculiar places, as though the hands of men had investigated there. Otherwise the wooden woman was very real in her occupation of the desolate beach. She made no protest at the desecration of men approaching her nudity.

"We call her Miss Neptune," Steven said.

Adie investigated with silent curiosity. The boy stood looking at the figurehead for so long a time that it was embarrassing. Finally Steven said, "You seen enough."

Adie started guiltily, and stole a glance at Steven.

"You ain't old enough for such things," Steven told him, taking up their way again.

As they left Miss Neptune behind, Adie said in a small voice, "I didn't mean anything. She's pretty."

"Maybe she is," Steven said shortly.

They walked on for some time before Adie asked, as if mischievously, "Do you look at her much?"

"Now see here . . ." Steven began. "You forget about that."

He frowned as he sensed Adie watching him. When Steven had first discovered the figurehead he couldn't bring himself to examine it, especially after Jesse's remarks about it. Later, he did. From it Steven learned things he had never known exactly before. Doc had once tried to tell him some of the same things, but had failed miserably. The figurehead, without the breath of life in it, was Steven's first wholesome contact with a woman.

The sun was firing the Everglades a blood red when they made camp for the night high on the beach. Here tiny sand flowers grew delicately, asking little moisture, seeming to exist on thin air. Goat's foot crisscrossed, weaving designs and patterns, and offered for admiration purple blossoms and tremendous green pods. The spot was far enough from the water not to be affected by its dampness, and not far enough on the land to get its dew. Normally, without a heavy wind, it was drier than most houses.

Steven led Adie once more through the scrub in back of the beach. After thirty yards, they came out on a dark stream, paralleling the beach and flowing south. They waded into the narrow river and scooped the cups they brought with them. The water, looking dirty and brown, was clear in the cups and fresh.

"I'll show you oysters growing on trees," Steven instructed. They went to thick bushes whose roots reached out of the water. Clustered to the roots, both above and below the surface, were myriads of oysters. Steven stopped and indicated to Adie that he should remain silent and watch.

In the water there was a swirl. A fish with no teeth but iron-hard jaws took the edge of one of the oysters in its mouth. There was a dull cracking sound. The oyster shell collapsed, and the fish nibbled at the succulence within.

Across the river there appeared a dozen small deer. Some stood on the bank to drink, others waded in. Steven grasped Adie's arm and nodded ever so slightly to denote their presence. The deer either caught the movement, or just then the human scent reached them, for with a furious, quick little gallop they darted away, sloshing the water. At the same time the fish disappeared.

The oysters they picked, roasted in the coals of their fire

with two of the sweet potatoes, were fat and delicious. To salt them they licked the deposit remaining on the backs of their hands from the ocean spray. The potatoes were rich and sweet, and with satisfaction Steven watched Adie devour his and pronounce it the best he ever had. They ate the rest of the fish, and had coffee and biscuits again. Only after the meal did the boy show any evidence of being tired. His eyelids drooped, waving his lashes, and his head nodded.

Steven didn't at once suggest that they sleep. He had waited for the boy to speak of himself, and thought he still might. Adie sat as if frightened again, for when his eyes closed sleepily, he tried to hold them open, fighting to remain awake. Still he said nothing, and finally Steven set the example of stretching out in the starlight.

Almost at once there came from the boy the long, regular respiration of sleep. He wasn't pretending now. Steven himself stayed awake for some time. He felt angry and had the impulse to shake Adie and demand of him to tell his story more fully. He was bothered by his small companion offering nothing at all.

He was a curious boy in more ways than one. He went off in the scrub by himself, out of sight, to perform his personal necessities. Steven had noted this as being unusual, for men together rarely followed the practice. Respecting the young delicacy, Steven had himself followed it.

Adie didn't skip stones. All day long he hadn't picked up a single stone to send across the water. Steven remembered how he, at Adie's age, had spent hours at this. Adie's fear one moment, and his complete lack of it the next, was strange, too. A few times Steven had sensed that the boy was afraid of him, or at least tensed against him. At other times he felt almost as though the boy was laughing at him for some reason. Wondering, Steven fell off to sleep.

He was awakened by a shrill scream. The next instant Adie was in his arms, twisted sideways, flinging himself at him in terror. Dazed, Steven made out dim black shapes down the beach. Recognition that they were bears came to him at the same instant he knew something else.

He was paralyzed to feel, beneath Adie's shirt, the same things that were to be seen on the ship's figurehead.

He gasped. He managed to get out, "It ain't anything." He loosened himself frantically, pushing Adie away. He reached blindly about, clawing at the sand. His fingers found pieces of shell, one stone. He threw them at the bears, which ambled off.

Steven kicked at the fire. It sprang up. Without thinking further, he reached toward Adie and snatched. The cap came away in his hand, and then, in place of it, was a cascade of fine hair, the color of a freshly shucked coconut. It shone in the licking flames of the fire.

They stared at each other. Steven felt the blood rush to his face. He was scarlet with shock and shame. The greatest horror, yet the greatest interest he had ever felt in his life, came over him.

He remembered how Adie's eyes had looked so soft and innocent. He remembered his thoughts before he went to sleep. In a revealing flash he recalled Adie's hesitancy when they reached the beach that morning, the first reluctance at catching fish with bare hands, the unwillingness to leave the regular route and go to Hypoluxo, Gerald's remark that there was something queer about the boy.

The rounded calves with little hard muscle on them, the short steps, the girlish giggle most of all, should have told him.

He had failed to suspect it because he was looking for something else. It explained Adie's keeping out of sight at the store as much as possible so as not to give herself away. Steven saw now why she had sneaked to Quimby's—both not to show herself and to see more of what sort of a person he was who would take her along the beach.

Adie, after being sure that the bears were gone, made a single comment. It was a combined exclamation and prayer. "Holy mother of smoke!"

Her voice sounded different already. It was not that of a boy which had yet to change, but that of a girl.

Steven asked, sounding hoarsely foolish to himself, "How old are you?"

"Going on nineteen."

Steven groaned. His sound was of acute physical pain. He had hoped she might not be a grown woman. His hands, with the recollection of what they had touched, seemed to burn. He realized that he was on his knees. Weakly, he sank back on the sand.

Adie, who sat with her legs under her, said in a rush, "I didn't lie to you. My name's Adela and I'm called Adie for short, and my mother's sick and I left school." She sounded contrite, excited, and fearful all at the same time.

Steven couldn't bring himself to say anything more. He could barely look at Adie in the new and acutely disturbing gender she had taken on. Usually he was filled with confusion when he saw a woman's stockinged ankle above her shoe top. He stole a furtive glance at Adie's breeches, and then gazed away. Now that she was a woman even seemed to make Adie herself conscious of her attire, for she shrank back a little.

"I didn't want to fool you," she went on. She both explained and defended herself. "I had to do it. I didn't have enough money to travel like a woman."

When Steven still didn't say anything, Adie was silent for a moment. Then, to make it worse, she began to sniffle.

Steven, alarmed, found his voice. "Don't do that," he said gruffly. "It's bad enough as it is." He realized he still held her cap in his hands. He flung it at her.

Adie's sniffles stopped. She took the cap and started to re-place it on her head, lifting up one side of her hair. Then she dropped it and let the cap remain on her lap.

"You're mad at me," she stated.

"I don't guess you know what you done."

"I didn't think I'd be found out. Not until after we got to Miami."

"What about then? Folks would think . . ."

"Not if you didn't know."

Steven didn't care to contemplate the fact that now he knew. He thought of something else. "It will be just as bad going back as it will be on. And the mail's got to be delivered."

"I want really to get to my mother," she related. "I didn't ever like it at the academy. For young ladies," she elucidated. "If the girls could see me now." She giggled.

Steven resented her laughter. "That ain't anything compared to Miami when it sees you. And me."

"There's no reason for a fuss," she said. "Aren't you—well, from the way you act—scared of girls?" She spoke uncertainly but hopefully, and seemed relieved when Steven answered:

"I don't see how that matters."

"If people know that," she argued, "they'll know it was all right with us." She appeared anxious to establish this point. "And my mother can tell."

"It'll be all right," he assured her. "But you got a pa as well as a ma."

"I'll talk to him, tell him."

"You better."

"Are you afraid of him?"

"I'm afraid of the ideas that're going to come in his head. I don't see why you picked my first trip alone for this." He was still aghast.

"I'm sorry. I really am. I'll do everything I can to fix it. I'll take all the blame."

He didn't want to talk about it any more, and hardly listened while Adie went on, finally, to tell about herself.

She and her people came from Ohio. Her mother, ailing, had been advised to live in a more temperate climate. They learned about Florida, and started out. In St. Augustine, when they found out there was no school in Miami, to which they had decided to go, she was left behind for the winter. Her folks continued on by steamer to Key West and then back up to Miami by schooner. When she decided to join them she obtained her boy's clothes from the son of the academy's gardener.

After awhile Adie stopped speaking. She slept almost immediately. Steven wondered how she could, and hated her for it. For a long time he himself didn't sleep. He lay on the sand, on the opposite side of the now dead fire from her, his eyes wide open, the soft breaking of the water on the shore like a crash in his ears.

Six

IN THE MORNING, when Steven awakened, Adie was gone. He sat up quickly, looking about. In both directions the beach was deserted.

He jumped to his feet, alarmed. He thought she might have walked on, alone. He thought that even as a girl there was, after all, something wrong with her.

His fright then was for the mail. But he saw his sack intact, where his head had rested on it for a pillow and for protection.

Searching, he discovered the imprint of Adie's feet. They led away, up into the scrub. Then he realized.

Another alarm came to him. Even as he had it, he wondered why he should feel so concerned about her. He should be wishing that something would happen to her. Instead, he called to the scrub, "Keep your eye out for snakes. You see one with lots of color in it, you get away from it."

An answering, unintelligible mumble came back. Steven made his own way to the brush, some distance away, for fear she might return and see him in the open. When he was concealed, in the middle of his own activity, he called again, "Don't stand under a coco; a nut can fall on you."

She was back on the beach when he returned. She had a fire going and the coffee-boil on, filled with water. Evidently she had taken it with her and back to the river, to fill. Her eagerness to please him allayed Steven's uneasiness not at all.

On her knees, she looked up at him once. Steven didn't look at her directly. He was merely acutely aware of her. He busied himself with breakfast. Neither of them seemed to find anything to say beyond the exchange having to do with the preparation of the food.

Adie ate with appetite and relish. Steven was not hungry. No bite seemed to want to go down at all. Afterward, when they packed, Adie said, as if it were a rehearsed speech:

"I won't be in your way. I won't bother you. I'll walk in back of you if it troubles you seeing me."

He looked at her to see if she was as humble as she sounded. She appeared to be sincere. And being so, he didn't want her to feel that he was that much inexperienced with women. "You don't have to do that," he said. "But you better put your cap back on and keep being a boy in case we see the combers."

Her eyes went wide, as they did for an instant when she took in something that startled her. But she said nothing about it. Instead, she stared down at the remains of her paper nautilus which had been crushed by her wild leap at him in the night. "Maybe you'll find another," Steven told her.

The girl walked as the boy had yesterday, easily. Steven kept his eyes high, over her slim shoulders, away from her bare limbs. He tried to hold his glance so that it did not include her hips. It was difficult. The gentle curves there, drawing his new knowledge of her, could not entirely be concealed by her breeches.

He wondered what kind of a girl she was to make her way in such a manner. He tried to deprecate her, make her cheap. But he knew she wasn't. He even had a secret admiration for her pluck. It had taken nerve to do it. Not every young girl would be courageous enough to set out with Cap Jim and Gerald, to say nothing of spending three days and two nights on a lonely beach with a strange man.

Steven remained appalled. The touch of her in his arms, the shock of her body pressed against his, were still with him. He couldn't get over how she looked without the cap on her head. That she was pretty, he couldn't deny. That there was something about the neatness of her face, about the loveliness of her reddish hair that he had always pictured somewhere in his mind, confused him. Yet there was no eagerness at seeing them, only a fright at the circumstances that made him shiver in the hot sun.

They marched silently, almost grimly. Before noon they came to Hillsborough. You could tell it from far away by the great trees its water nurtured. There were gray cypresses thicker than a barrel, lofty pines, and great banyans whose ropelike air roots dropped to the ground from high overhead. Matching their activity even more dramatically, red mangroves reached a hundred feet into the air, their roots arching thirty feet in all directions to join trunks that were headed for the sea, leaving on their trail a mass of dead and dying wood. The dissolute habit of the growth made it look like a depraved giant shedding clothes behind him.

Orchids and other air plants roosted like chickens on weird branches. Aerial fungi and lichens peered from the creepers. Here and there vivid tree snails clung coyly between twisting stems. Velvet seeds were dropped to the ground in a reckless planting whose waste seemed to boast of the magnificent profundity of life.

Through the maze of growth there ran a liquid lane of water perhaps two hundred feet wide that emptied itself into the sea. Beyond its mouth was a bar on which waves broke their backs.

Adie said nothing for a moment while she gazed about. She plucked a red-striped snail from the bark of a magnolia. She looked at Steven. He offered no information about the wildness here. In a piqued tone she inquired, "How do we get across?"

He strode to the bank of a river, pushing aside branches. Here, snugly nesting, was a flat-bottomed skiff. Steven untied it and shipped the oars. He told Adie to get in and then followed her.

In the middle of the stream, in the shade of the towering trees, there came a sharp snap of jaws rending wood. Adie was looking the other way, but she whirled at the sound to ask, "What was that?"

"Alligator," said Steven. He held the oar out of water. Fresh wood showed where one corner had been broken off.

Adie went white. Her fright made Steven feel a little better. He regained some of his composure when he told her, "Ain't no danger now. It's only after the rains. Then the stream runs hard and fish come in. The gators boil up, along with sharks and barracuda."

It was back of the next ten-mile stretch where the beachcombers lived. Steven didn't tell Adie. He didn't want to frighten her any more. And he didn't expect to see the combers. They rarely happened to be out except when the northeasters beat up for days or the big blows came from the southeast.

This time he was mistaken. He saw the figures down the beach, standing to their waists in the water, before Adie was aware of them. His heart gave a jump, not for himself, but because of the girl. He felt a responsibility; that he blamed her for it made it none the less real. He told her quietly, "Let me do the talking to them."

He caught up, and walked by her side. "Don't look so scared," he said. She nodded, her eyes fixed on the three men. Steven had hoped they were busy with wreckage that would keep them interested. He saw that they were fishing. One twirled a weighted line about his head, then slung it into the sea. After the throw he looked around, saw them coming, and spoke to his companions.

All three backed up, letting out their lines as Steven and Adie came along.

"Howdy, Theron," Steven said. He spoke to the largest of the men. Theron had a short beard and bushy dark eyebrows. He was stripped to the waist, baring a broad torso. To the other two, whose names Steven didn't know, he nodded.

Cheerily, Theron wanted to know, "Where's Paget?"

"I'm carrying the mail alone from now on."

"That so?" inquired Theron. With the other two he eyed Steven's haversack.

"That's so," Steven told him evenly.

Theron laughed. "You sound like you're suspicious of us."

Ordinarily, Steven could have answered in the same cajoling spirit. But Adie's presence made him altogether serious. "I know nobody would be crazy enough to touch the mail."

They didn't comment on this. The smallest of the men, a thin creature in a tattered shirt, indicated Adie and inquired, "Who's your passenger?"

"A kid going to his folks."

The beachcombers stared at Adie. She stared back silently.

"Can't he talk?" Theron asked.

Steven tensed.

"Sure I can talk," Adie answered. "What are you catching?"

"Pompano," the third man told her.

The ease with which Adie spoke made Steven relax. "You getting any, we could do with one," he proposed.

Theron gave his line to the small man and dug in the damp sand. He uncovered a shallow trench filled with closely packed fish. He picked one out, cleaned the sand from it in the wash of a wave, and handed it to Steven.

Steven was in no hurry now. That would be the worst thing to show. "How's the pluming?" he asked.

They regarded him with narrowed eyes. Theron asked, "You ain't looking after the government about that, Pierton?"

"I'm just practicing for when I do."

One of the men grinned and said, "We're doing all right."

Steven became even bolder. He glanced across the beach and observed, "I never see any place you live."

Theron hawed. "You'd look a long ways before you found it."

"I'll come looking some day," Steven promised. "I'll go upcountry and get a U. S. marshal and bring him, too."

They laughed. Steven walked on with Adie. When they were out of earshot she said, "My heart's still beating three times too fast."

"It can't be anything to what mine was doing at first. You answered them right."

She gave him a sidelong look. "You talked to them yourself."

Steven was oblivious to the admiration in her tone. He was still too filled with relief to get her safely past the combers.

The constraint between them was not removed. Even the sight at New River did not affect it, though Steven told her a little more about the second inlet. "Back up there is what's left of Fort Lauderdale," he said. "They used it in the Seminole War. You can't see it," he instructed as Adie peered. "That there creeping and twisting across there," he explained as they climbed into the skiff, "is the tree-that-walks."

The mahoe grew on the far bank above the landing to which he rowed. It reared upward for about ten feet and then, as if tired, drooped to the ground, where it grew up again. It continued this process over a large area, doubling back on itself. The maze of crooked, overhanging limbs coiled and writhed about like so many colossal serpents. Trumpet-shaped lemon blossoms blazed between round heavy glossy green leaves so thick that there was only twilight beneath them.

That night they had pompano with the potatoes. Steven cut off the tops of green coconuts for the soft fresh fruit, and bored fully ripened nuts for the milk. Adie watched the preparations hungrily, helping when she could, when he allowed her. Her eyes lighted as they met his, inviting him to be friends.

He looked away, not knowing how to deal with her. All day long he had been thinking of the things he told her in the house at Hypoluxo. He had been amazed, then, that he could say them. Now they filled him with chagrin. That he had expressed them, not knowing that Adie was a woman, made him angry. That, above all, made him feel how much she had tricked him. She was sure to make fun of him later about it, holding up his naked feelings to ridicule, and telling others. He was certain that he despised her.

Seven

ADIE DIDN'T SAY MUCH until they were ready for sleep. Carefully, Steven let her choose her side of the fire. He stretched out on the other side. The sea breathed before them. Above, the stars were glitteringly white. Back in the scrub animals moved and sometimes called. Once there came the shriek of a wildcat.

"I'm not afraid any more," Adie announced. "At least, not so much."

"There's nothing to be afraid of," Steven told her. He didn't know if she referred to him, or to the country, or perhaps both.

"It was only because at first it was new and funny," she went on. "And I had to keep pretending I was a boy, and was scared you'd find out I wasn't."

Steven didn't answer.

"I like it now," she said.

The soft night enclosed them, each in his own place, close, yet far apart. The coals of the fire, like a red warning representing all their differences, separated them.

He heard Adie sigh. She sounded content when she asked, "Is it always like this?"

"Mostly."

"What do you do when it rains?"

"Get wet." Steven fought with himself not to be antagonistic to her. Strangely, here in the night, he didn't want to be. Yet he couldn't prevent himself.

"Aren't there places you can get under?" she wanted to know.

"There's caves if you happen to be near them." He could have told her more, how he built a shelter of palm fronds, how the vegetation in places was thick enough to keep you dry. But he wanted no more to reveal any part of himself. Until he knew how she was going to act about his confession in regard to a wife he shrank from risking more.

Adie tried a new subject. "It's a good thing we got past the beachcombers."

"Maybe you don't know how good it was," Steven informed her.

"What would have happened," she asked, "if they'd found out about me?"

"I don't know exactly. Maybe nothing. But probably there'd been a fight. With three against one I expect I'd lost."

She thought that over, then observed, "I don't think they've got any women."

"How can you tell?"

"I just think that."

Steven knew he shouldn't rub it in. But he said, "They came pretty close to getting one."

"You're still mad at me," she said. "I don't blame you. I'd be a lot madder than you are."

Steven said nothing. She was silent.

He thought she slept, when he heard her voice again. "Do you know how to dance?" she asked.

Startled at her question, Steven replied, "They have a play sometimes, with pretty good fiddlers, and I go."

She made no comment.

Steven was consumed with curiosity. He raged at himself for having it, was furious when he had to inquire, "What did you ask that for?"

Sleepily, she answered, "I was just wondering."

Again Steven had the uncomfortable impression that she was laughing at him. Only now she laughed not as a boy, but as a woman. The fact of her sex he could not surmount nor erase. It was like a deep burn.

In the morning Adie asked no more personal questions. She seemed to avoid them. When Steven was sure this was her intent he was more at ease for the day ahead. He tried to forget what lay at the other end. Considerately, he even brought himself to look at her graceful little feet and ask, "They holding out?"

"They're getting hard on the sand. I always wanted to go barefoot."

Sandpipers performed ahead of them. The birds accompanied them south, pursuing the waves as they went, nimbly and daintily following the water back and forth, continually pecking a minute life they found to eat, never wetting their feet and leaving spidery tracks. The beach began to flatten out and broaden, until there was barely any slant to it. At the same time the ocean shallowed, the bottom possible to see far out. Adie, glancing back, stopped and said, "That's darker than a cloud."

Close to the shore, stretching as far up the coast as the eye could see, and perhaps fifty feet wide, was a black carpet of fish moving just under the surface. Steven was surprised that the girl, so soon, could distinguish the difference between it and the shadows of clouds that, moving over the water, looked a great deal like it.

"Mullet," he told Adie, "a big school. Watch!" he cried.

One section of the moving carpet leaped to quicker life. Myriads of fish began to jump and dart about. The school broke into two parts as larger fish streaked in toward the beach. Back along the greater part of the school an instantaneous message flashed. It hesitated and then came to a stop without bunching. The smaller portion kept on, until it was opposite Steven and Adie.

Now the larger fish could be made out to be jacks. Savagely they attacked and devoured, working their lively dinners almost to the shore. Then the jacks were gone, as suddenly as they appeared. The two parts of the magic carpet joined again, and once more the whole slowly flowed south.

It took the school an hour to pass Adie and Steven as they continued on their way. Twice more was it attacked and broken, but each time irrevocably, minus an unnoticeable fraction of its members, it made its deliberate, mysterious way on. Adie said, in awe, "I never thought there were that many fish in the whole ocean."

"Sometimes," Steven told her, "I see two or three bunches like that in a day. You see other kinds, too. There's been runs of mackerel that look like they cover the whole sea. You could almost walk on them. Porpoises cut in them, chasing them until they jump out on the beach, hundreds of them."

He stopped, realizing that he was speaking again enthusiastically to her, giving her a part of his life.

But in this, dealing with the natural things of the beach, he could see no harm. She appeared to have a feeling for them herself. Not everyone appreciated them. He felt almost glad that he could impart something of them to her, a woman. He had a confidence he had never experienced before. He had shown her things when she was a boy; now he could offer his exhibits to her as a female.

He waited until Adie saw it herself and they came up to it at noon to explain about the drinking barrel he and Jesse had arranged on the beach. Above high-tide mark a barrel stood on its end. Fastened over its open lip and protruding all around it, extended lengths of broad bamboo split in half. Catching water when it rained, these deposited it with the catch of the barrel itself.

Steven dipped the tin cups while he related, "There ain't any fresh water for miles up and down here, because it's mostly salt mangrove back inland. This is the only thing that's been put up for sailors wrecked along the shore."

Adie looked over the rim of her cup as she drank, her gray eyes squinting only a little in the beating sunlight. She read a crude sign standing a few feet from the barrel. A piece of driftwood had been driven into the sand. Nailed against this was a pointed board on which had been printed with a charred stick the words, "Miami 11 mi." Below this sign, another board pointed across the beach.

Steven showed her what that meant. They had their own lunch from the tree that grew well back of the beach, protected on all sides by the profuse vegetation. The eggfruit tree grew twenty feet high, and from it there hung yellow and orange fruit the size of a fist.

Steven let Adie pick her own. They peeled off the thin, papery covering to reach the mealy interior pulp resembling the dark-boiled yolk of an egg. The flavor, sweet and musty, was also rich and cloying. It was a favorite with Steven, but he had yet to find anyone else who liked it. Adie did, eating one after another.

Deeper in the brush, a curious, sharp trumpet sound was repeated shrilly. When Steven saw the fascinated look on Adie's face, he led her toward it. He cautioned her to creep the final few yards toward the spot from where the calls came.

They peered through the bushes. Five sandhill cranes pranced about the roots of a gumbo limbo. They stood six feet tall and were steel-blue in color. One dug with his oversize beak in the ground around the tree. The others jumped about impatiently, shrieking like frolicsome children. Then they all pecked at the findings. Another took up the work, while the first worker joined the trumpeting and ungainly dancing.

They all stopped suddenly and held their heads to one side in a listening attitude. Curious, they advanced on Steven and

Adie. Steven moved only his lips to advise Adie to remain perfectly still.

The great cranes came to within ten yards of them. The birds looked them over carefully. They seemed to confer, find the two humans satisfactory, and then went back to the gumbo limbo, prancing to it awkwardly but proudly. The trumpet call came again, as though sounding the celebration of a brave feat.

Steven had to drag Adie away from the sight. They were both laughing and Steven said, "They're a curiosity in this world."

"I'd like to be a man," Adie declared, "and walk the beach all the time."

The reference to her being male brought unpleasant recollection. It affected Steven's part of their genial association. He became glum thinking of the reception awaiting him. Adie seemed to sense his attitude, and regretfully accept it. They settled down to the business of covering the last miles.

It was late afternoon when they reached the outer beach across the bay from Miami. Here was a fetid swamp of tangled bush mangrove, thick with mosquitoes and sandflies. Little was left of the coconut plantation once established, only to fail when armies of huge rats destroyed the seedlings. Wild pigs crashed in the scrub, grunting and snorting. The ferocious boars sometimes fought panthers.

Steven and Adie pushed into the growth along a soggy black path. She clung close to his heels, yelping with pain when several times sandspurs found her flesh. It was a relief to both of them when they stood on the inner shore.

Adie looked for the town across the wide green-blue bay.

"There ain't enough of it to see from here," Steven told her.

They found and got in the boat. Steven began rowing. Adie, sitting in the stern, was excited rather than disturbed by what lay ahead. She was subdued one moment, and Steven sensed that this was for his sake; at other moments she chattered about the trip. She took out some of her shell treasures and looked at them. She hadn't found another nautilus and now she asked, "When you see one will you bring it to me?"

Steven nodded. She became silent, respecting his apprehension of what faced him in Miami. He knew how his manner again reproached her. But he couldn't help it. He sweated at the prospect of how people were going to receive them, from the rowing, and from having her so close before him in the boat.

To cool himself he stopped, near the middle of the bay, at an odd structure built on three pilings. A platform was suspended between these and on it was a brass-hooped barrel connected with a pipe that led down into the salt water. The liquid in the barrel, however, was fresh when they drank it. A spring on the bottom of the bay had been tapped.

Adie took out her silver dollar and tendered it to Steven, her eyes dancing. When he shook his head, and started to row again she looked tremulous.

The mouth of the Miami River was fifty yards across, and from it emerged a slow deep stream. On the north point was a big cluster of coconut palms. Seen between their trunks was the long low gray coquina building that once served as the barracks of old Fort Dallas; now it was the Dade County Courthouse. A few houses stood some distance away, mostly of cabbage construction, but the main settlement was on the south point of the river.

Here, set back from the bank, was Bunnell's Trading Post. It boasted white paint on an entirely frame structure; extravagantly, it had shingles. A warehouse stood beside it. Near by, a conglomeration of structures peeped from the thick foliage. Some were all cabbage, some were driftwood with thatched roofs, a few were constructed of milled lumber with cabbage covering them, others had frame sides with a canvas top, and there were half a dozen tents.

There was no discernible street. The houses were placed at odd angles to each other, wherever their owners happened to choose to build. The community had a careless air about it, looking a little pitiful, a little courageous.

At the shore, before the trading post, a stubby dock led into the river. On the bank were drawn up dugout canoes, near which were the temporary camps of a number of Seminoles. Fires, made by arranging logs in the form of the spokes of a wheel, burned here. Dark faces peered below elaborately bright turbans of the men and above necklaces piled to the chins of the Indian women. They were the only people to be seen.

Steven banged the dock with the rowboat and tied up while still sitting at the oars. He hadn't yet worked out how he would reveal Adie to the community.

She decided it for him. Breathlessly, she asked, "Do you know where my folks live?"

Steven pointed up the river on the south side. "A quarter of a mile along there through the palm woods," he murmured.

Adie glanced once at the trees and bushes shutting off the home she had never seen. "I'll keep it a secret," she announced suddenly, "about what you said at Hypoluxo. I won't even tell anybody about the island. And I hope you find the kind of wife you want."

Before Steven realized what was happening, she leaned forward. Like a sweet eddy of air her lips touched his for a fleeting instant. Then she was out of the boat and running up the dock.

Eight

STEVEN SAT STUNNED. The touch of her lips, giving him his first kiss, was fresh and tenuous. It darted in before it was to be seen, was gone almost before it could be known it had been there. What it left behind jolted and quickened him. There flashed through him, wildly, the knowledge that her action was impulsively expressed gratitude for bringing her along the beach without harm.

His own lips felt as if they were on fire. His whole face suffused red. He looked quickly at the Indians to see if they had observed. He knew some of them. But none of them showed any evidence of having seen.

Steven sat there until he believed his face had returned to normal. Then he picked up his sack from the bottom of the boat and made his way to the trading post. He exchanged greetings with some of the Indians. To try to compose himself further, he inquired for one of them. He was curious about where the beachcombers hid out, and he believed his friend Charming Tiger might be able to tell him. But his inquiry brought the response, "Tiger no come now."

In the store Dan Bunnell was dealing with a tall, solemn Indian. The fat trader looked up from behind his counter and said, "You look like taking on the job is too much for you, Stevie. What you seen, a ghost?"

"I reckon it was just hot coming across the bay."

Bunnell looked at him curiously. While he went on with his trading, Steven took out the mail bag, watching what the Indian offered. On the counter crawled a dozen tiny turtles. Bunnell gave the man a few small coins for them and then said, "Take them out and throw them in the river." When the

Indian didn't understand, Bunnell repeated it loudly, with gestures. Contentedly, the Indian picked up the turtles and went out.

"Got to buy useless stuff like that from them," Bunnell complained disgustedly, "or they get mad. Then I don't get their skins." He pointed to a thick pile of furs lying on a board set across the top of a barrel. "You ever see such otter as that?"

"I expect not."

"What's the matter with you, Stevie?"

Steven swallowed. He wanted to tell the trader, but didn't know just how to broach it. Adie's kiss had made it more difficult. He lifted his cap from his head and stood there saying nothing.

"You eat something that don't agree with you?" Bunnell asked.

"It ain't that. It's . . ." The words stuck in his throat at the laughter he knew would follow their utterance.

"I guess you just miss Jesse on the trip and got lonesome," Bunnell chuckled. "You'll get over it. Bringing a passenger sometimes will help."

Steven choked and agreed to this. Carrying his haversack, he escaped from the store, going out a side door leading to the rest of the building. Bunnell called after him, but he paid no attention.

Steven came to the rooms the trader rented to newcomers or travelers. They were stifling, boxlike affairs, and one was set aside for the mail carrier when he stayed in Miami overnight.

He flung himself on the narrow cot. Despairingly, he decided to let them find out as they would. It couldn't be much worse no matter how it was discovered.

Dozing in his misery, Steven heard people coming in for their mail. A new voice spoke. Then there was a shout. Guffaws followed.

Steven heard the sound of footsteps coming his way. In the open doorway Bunnell appeared. Beside his chubby face others looked in, grinning broadly.

"I found out what's biting you," the trader announced. "Looks like you'll have to marry her!" he cried.

The faces grimaced and roared with laughter. Steven glared bleakly.

"If it was anybody except Stevie," another said, "her pa would be coming to see him with a shotgun."

"I hear he's coming anyway."

After a time they went away. A few more came, made their remarks and left. The voices in the store rose, then suddenly fell silent.

Steven now heard steady, firm steps. They seemed to have purpose in them. He knew to whom they belonged. He wondered if it were true that he would have to marry Adie. The thought seemed to draw the blood from his entire body. He half rose, to sit on the edge of the bed.

A slight, middle-aged man stood in the doorway. His hair was graying and about the corners of his eyes there were crinkles. His gaze bored into Steven, and Steven stared back steadily.

The gray eyes, so much like Adie's, finally made a decision. The man said, "I'm glad I knew you before. And that I've heard of you a good deal. Mrs. Titus and I want to thank you for bringing Adela safely."

The only thing Steven could think of to say was, "Yes, sir."

"Any blame connected with this," Titus went on, "we realize is to be placed upon Adela. She has explained how it occurred."

At least she had kept her word.

"And we realize," her father went on, "that your conduct has been honorable."

When Steven nodded with relief and got to his feet, Titus shook his hand warmly. "What is to be done with her," he went on, "we don't yet know. It has happened too suddenly."

Steven had a feeling of panic, which he didn't attempt to understand, that Adie might be sent back to school in St. Augustine.

"Will you," Titus asked, "do us the honor of taking supper with us, so that Mrs. Titus and I can show our full appreciation?"

Steven demurred. At his hesitancy the older man went on, "I might say also, though it is not essential, that this would help the situation. There is bound to be gossip, even though good-natured and innocent."

"I got to clean up first."

"We shall await you, then. And again, thank you, my boy." Titus walked down the hall.

The father's formal words were almost as disturbing as the daughter's behavior. But at them both Steven found himself several times smiling as he shaved and arranged his appearance.

Once ready, however, he found he couldn't bring himself to go. Titus, he was sure, didn't know anything about the kiss. The man hadn't taken care of that with his phrases. At the prospect of facing Adie, at least so soon after that feathery touch on his lips, Steven quailed.

Yet he had agreed to go. He waited until the store had cleared and then went out. Bunnell greeted him uproariously, "I hear you got a reprieve. It's lucky the Tituses are the kind of folks they are. If they wasn't you'd be on your way to a preacher right now!"

Steven started through the quick twilight to the Titus place. He passed the houses of the main settlement and came out on a rutted sand path leading through the palm and pine woods. On this, as he neared his destination, his feet began to drag.

He stopped, to think it out. Tingling him as much as the kiss was what Adie had said about keeping Hypoluxo a secret. That was so unexpected, so startling, that he couldn't yet adjust himself to it. He remembered his own words, what he had told her on the island. He wondered if she actually meant her assurance about them, or if she merely mocked him. He couldn't be sure. He wished, painfully, he knew the ways of women better. All he could do was to torture himself.

He turned. He couldn't bring himself to go and face Adie

with her family. And he couldn't eat at Bunnell's table, either, to listen to the trader's chiding and that of his two sisters who kept house for him.

He made his way back, around to the right of the houses, avoiding a tent set off by itself. He wandered aimlessly until he came to the bay shore. Here he sat under a coconut, not caring if any of the heavy nuts dropped to fall on him. He thought of walking down to the settlement at Coconut Grove and getting supper there. But he didn't feel hungry at all.

Darkness came and still he sat, staring out over the placid water. Fowey Light gave a dull gleam in the southeast beyond Cape Florida. The Key West mail and supply schooner slid up the bay and around the point to the dock, stirring phosphorus as it passed; it was late. A school of mullet leaped abruptly, small darts shooting repeatedly out of the water as something below pursued them. A sea cow nosed up to breathe noisily and far out a tarpon rolled lazily.

In the morning, his haversack packed with the upgoing mail, Steven felt foolish. He told himself that a grown man would never act the way he did. He had to make amends, to the Tituses, to himself.

He forced his feet to take the path to their place. He met only two men on the way. One, crossing the path, shouted to him. The other, passing him, clouted him on the back heartily.

The Titus house, set on the edge of a partially cleared homestead, was half board and batten and half thatch, in two sections, one having been built after the other. The frame part was on the front, across which ran an open, covered porch.

Steven approached cautiously. At the far side of the house he saw Mr. Titus working at his coontie mill. Around and around he pushed a grinding cylinder placed under a hopper. The pulp was later rallied in a retort, partly settled, and then the starch run off into tanks for final settling. Dried in the sun on cloth-covered frames, five barrels of roots made a barrel of starch worth in Key West from three to five cents a pound. Flour was also made from the wild coontie plant which grew, according to the Indians, in the footsteps of God who had once passed this way.

Steven drew back from the sight of Adie's father, and slowly mounted the porch. His knock was tentative, and he wasn't prepared for the almost instant answer.

Adie stood in the doorway. At first he didn't recognize her at all. Gone were the breeches and shirt. In their places was a ruffled, puce-colored dress that reached within an inch of the the floor. Her small white well-formed feet were no longer in evidence, but withdrawn into shoes. Her hair had been piled on top of her head in a soft pompadour. There was now no semblance of a boy about her; she was all woman.

Her mouth twitched when she said, "You're a little late for supper."

It wouldn't have been so bad if she wasn't changed so much. He could only stare until she laughed and then he said, quickly, in one breath, "I come to give my apology how's your ma?"

He didn't explain further. Adie seemed to know. Her eyes twinkled. "She's some better, thank you."

A weak voice called from inside. "Is that Mister Pierton? I'm sorry we can't ask you in at present. Please come again."

"Yes, Ma'm," Steven answered.

Adie came out a little way on the porch. "Was it bad, Steven?"

At her form of address he hitched the haversack on his back. He ran one finger across each side of his mustache and said, "Just about what you'd expect. I figure on living through it."

"You aren't mad at me any more?"

"Maybe not so much."

She looked at him gratefully. At her gaze and at the magical thing the dress did to her, Steven was seized with the memory of what she had done in the boat yesterday. He backed off the porch, saying, "It's time I was starting."

"You won't forget my nautilus?"

"I'll certain get you a big one."

"I'm not going back to school," she told him. "I'm staying here."

"That's first-rate!" he exclaimed. At his impetuosity, he began to stride away.

Her voice followed him down the path. "Remember me to Miss Neptune."

He stopped, and turned. She was smiling. After an instant he grinned back at her, first uncertainly, then with assurance. He wheeled, and went on.

$\mathcal{N}ine$

NEW LETTERING had been painted on the sign above the door of the store. "Palm Beach," it now read. Steven couldn't get used to the sight of it, nor to the thought that he had furnished the name. Jesse was in the store with Doc, waiting impatiently for him to arrive. Jesse would leave as soon as he had the Miami mail in his pouch, traveling at night. Tomorrow he would return with the northern mail for Steven to take on Monday.

Jesse stayed a little longer than it took to sort the mail when Steven told about his trip. Doc asked, "How'd the boy behave himself?"

It wasn't as difficult to tell them as Steven had imagined. There was an element of revealing an astounding story when he said, "It wasn't a he."

"Hah?" Doc questioned, peering above his spectacles.

"What're you talking about?" Jesse demanded.

"I said he turned out to be a female."

"I told you time and again," Doc lectured, "not to walk in

that sun without your cap on. Now I better fix you up something to take for—"

Steven reiterated his statement, and recounted the facts, or nearly all of them, about Adie.

When Doc believed him he cried, "I'll be blamed!"

Jesse howled. He couldn't stop, but went into paroxysms of laughter. Tears streamed merrily from his eyes as he choked, "Now you done it!"

"Done what?"

"You got a sweetheart."

"It ain't anything like that."

"Then I'd like to know what it is," Jesse exulted.

Doc nodded happily.

Jesse pestered him for details on how he found out about Adie. "Her cap blowing off don't sound like all of it to me," he suggested. "I'll bet there was more to it. And how did you get along about—"

"Now you look here, Jesse Paget," Doc scolded. "You got your woman. You get on. If you was in such a tarnation hurry before to get away so you can get back to her that much sooner, you're in just as much of a hurry now."

Jesse slung the mail bag over his shoulder. "I got to help Steve along in his romance," he said. "I don't know how he's going to handle himself without any experience."

Steven aimed a kick at him, which Jesse avoided. As he went out, Jesse called back, "Don't you forget to invite me and Della to the wedding. And Linda'll skin you alive if you don't have her right along on the honeymoon!"

Steven wondered if he could ever be with Adie the way Jesse was with Della. Perhaps not exactly the same way, but some of it. He envied the ease of their feeling for each other. The conviction came to him that in his thoughts about Adie during the last three days coming up the beach, he had been carried away. He felt far beyond himself.

Doc told him, "You're getting some pretty outlandish passengers your first trips."

Steven looked at him.

"There's another waiting," Doc revealed. "Been here two days, staying at the Thomas House. Name of Hurley, Sylvanus Hurley. Come in on a schooner that was going to Key West but had to turn back because her bottom was giving out. He's itching to go with you."

"What's wrong about that?" Steven wanted to know. "It's five dollars in my pocket if you told him the fare."

"I told him. But that ain't all. He's a boomer from the North. He tells everybody he's going to make Miami into a big city. They can have him down there. We don't want any land sharps around here."

Steven still waited for something really bad about the man.

"He's got a thousand dollars in cash on him," Doc said. "Rather, he's got it with me now, sending it registered mail. That means you'll carry it and be responsible."

"He can do that if he wants," said Steven.

"There's more yet," said Doc. "Two of them beachcombers was up here day before last."

Steven became still. "Which ones?"

"The one they call Theron, and a little fellow. Come buying some supplies."

"Did this Hurley—?"

"His mouth is open more than it's shut. Maybe he didn't know who the combers was, but they learned who he is."

"The money, too?"

"They left soon after they heard of the money."

Steven told of his meeting with the combers. He hadn't seen them coming back, and if they had been here two days ago this meant they had avoided him on the beach on his return trip. He didn't like that. "Still, it don't mean anything," he concluded. "They wouldn't try anything."

"Don't you be too sure," Doc warned.

He didn't see Sylvanus Hurley until Monday morning. The man who walked in carrying a bulky suitcase was younger than Steven had pictured. He could not be in his thirties. Steven guessed next door, twenty-nine. His face was smooth-shaven, handsome. His body was well formed and his coat fitted exactly over his checkered waistcoat. On his head a gray high-crowned bowler was clamped tightly.

He had an agreeable, attractive manner. Doc didn't greet him. Hurley introduced himself, holding out his hand to Steven and saying, "Obedience. You're the carrier?"

"Must be," said Steven, taking the hand.

"You're going to walk me?" Hurley's question was pleasant, but evidently he didn't expect an answer, for he turned to Doc and cheerily inquired, "Where's my money envelope?"

Doc glanced at him with distaste. "Right here," he told him. He pointed to an envelope on the counter. "Addressed to yourself: 'Sylvanus Hurley, Esquire, General Delivery, Miami, Registered Mail.' Just like you give it to me and just like you got the receipt for."

Sylvanus Hurley walked over to the letter, picked it up, examined its red wax seal, and then put it down again. "There's ten one-hundred-dollar bills in that," he said. "A thousand dollars in good American money. I'm holding the Post Office Department responsible."

"That means you, Stevie," Doc said. "He's held," he informed Hurley. "You know it. That's why you're doing it this way."

Sylvanus Hurley laughed. His laugh was infectious, winning. "I'm merely taking advantage of the services offered. Like any businessman."

Doc looked to Steven for him to say something. Steven found no dislike of the man, as he had expected. Sylvanus Hurley was ingratiating, a person most people would like.

Doc said, "Mister, if you hadn't opened your mouth so wide while waiting here, there wouldn't be any question of the beachcombers holding up your money. I still think you and it ought to wait over till a boat comes along."

"When will that be?" Sylvanus seemed to have no fear of

the beachcombers, but was simply interested in when he could make the trip.

"No telling exactly," Steven put in. "There ain't enough trade between the lake and Miami to make regular service worth the trouble. It might be a few days. It might be a week or a month. We'll come out all right on the beach—if you can give any account of yourself in case we got to."

"I'll do what I can." Sylvanus spoke as if a fight would be nothing new to him.

"Don't you see?" Doc demanded of Steven. "He can't lose even if his money is robbed. He's protected. You ain't."

"It's all right," Steven told him. "You carrying that grip?" he asked Sylvanus. He thought to warn him.

"I must have my belongings."

Doc eyed Sylvanus's suitcase as though taking enjoyment in some secret thought. "Here's his letter, Stevie," he said, "that he's put on you instead of carrying himself."

Steven put the registered letter with other papers inside the deep pocket of his shirt, buttoning the flap over it. Making a last adjustment of his shoulder straps, he nodded to Sylvanus, who picked up his bag and followed him out of the store.

On the beach, as he removed his shoes and rolled his trousers, he advised Sylvanus, "You best do the same. It's easier walking the sand barefoot."

"Better than having on your shoes?"

"For one thing, your feet slip in shoes and make blisters. For another thing, you can't keep the sand out of them. You want your pants rolled up, too, so they don't flap or get wet, and it's freer."

Sylvanus considered, watching Steven's preparations. He appraised the advice sharply and correctly. Besides removing his shoes he took off his coat and inserted it under the straps of his suitcase. This he shouldered.

Steven expected him to want to rest during the first mile. Sylvanus dripped with perspiration, but followed without faltering. He even began to talk. "I looked up the weather records before I came here. And do you know what they meant to me?"

He answered his own question, beginning a dissertation that made Steven think he was selling something.

"I could see from the bare records that you had the best climate in the world here. Climate's the thing, that's what I'm interested in. Take this beautiful sunny day with the blue sky and the breeze and the waving palm trees. The records didn't lie. This is the American Riviera. That's what it's going to be here, that's what I'm going to make it."

The man sounded so persuasive, and so positive, that Steven had to catch himself up from believing him.

"Why," Sylvanus went on, "it's a tropical paradise. "It's—" He searched for a term to fit his enthusiasm. "It's the Empire of the Sun. It's the Garden of Eden."

"The land's pretty good right along here by the coast," Steven told him, "but you go back about as far as you can spit and there you get it by the gallon instead of by the acre."

Sylvanus thrust this aside. "If it's a little damp," he proposed, "even a little wet, it can be drained."

"There's places back there," Steven said, "where if you wasn't forked with two legs you'd keep right on going down forever."

"No matter," Sylvanus went on breezily. "The land's good. Any land with this kind of sun on it is bound to be good."

"You're aiming to get some of it?" Steven inquired.

"Every inch I can lay my hands on. I'll start at Miami and work out from there." Sylvanus dropped his voice and confided, "Just between you and me, I advise you doing the same thing. Or any time you want a choice section you just come to me. . . ."

It tickled Steven that the man was selling land before he had seen or acquired it. He was a true boomer, all right. Steven was sure he gauged the other's temper correctly when he asked, "All this land you're going to get—you going to buy or steal it?"

Sylvanus laughed. "Steven, you malign me."

Steven admired the boomer's ready familiarity. He matched it by stopping and saying, "We better rest that grip of yours, Sylvanus."

Sylvanus let his suitcase down on the sand. He took off his bowler and wiped his streaming face with a huge blue handkerchief. "That's what I like to hear. Just because I've put you in the position of doing me an official service isn't any reason we can't be friends."

Steven decided that he didn't feel friendly enough toward Sylvanus to show him or tell him about Hypoluxo. The man's remarks about land made Steven chary of this. It would be better for him not to know of the island, and the informal status of its ownership.

He gave Sylvanus a good many opportunities to rest during the day. It was only toward evening that the boomer tired from carrying the suitcase and made his way doggedly, now silently. When they made camp for the night, he was exhausted. He was sunburned and his feet were slightly swollen. "Soak them in the ocean," Steven instructed. "I'll open a jelly-juicer to smear on that skin of yours, soft coconut meat being the best cooling thing for that."

More comfortable, with food in his stomach, and a greater respect in his eyes for the country and its distances, Sylvanus brought out cheroots and passed one to Steven. They smoked and talked about the beachcombers. Sylvanus listened care-fully.

Steven told him where he figured the attack, if it was to come, would occur. He expected the combers to find and row the skiff across either at Hillsborough or New River. They would count on him to swim alone across the river to get the boat and then attempt to jump him as he came, tired, from the water.

Sylvanus anticipated the plan Steven had to meet this. "We'll swim over together, with both of us ready for them," he proposed. He appeared almost eager for the meeting, no matter

how it might come about. He mused over it at some length before broaching another subject.

"Are there any pretty girls in Miami?"

"Well," Steven replied, "there's one I know of."

Sylvanus glanced at him. There was the hint, not the open
fact, of his amusement. "I can see how you feel about that
one." He blew several smoke rings, expertly. "I make it a point
myself," he said, "of never taking a woman seriously. If you
do that, you're lost from the beginning. Of course you've got
to pretend to. The amount of your success depends on how
well you can pretend."

He sounded as though he were giving instruction. Steven
thought he might get some pointers from him. He said, "I ain't
so good at that."

"I don't say it doesn't require practice," Sylvanus went on,
"perhaps a good deal of practice. But it's amazing, really amazing, how far a little flattery will go. That's the thing. A woman
will believe anything as long as it flatters her. Anything.
They're made for it. That's what you've got to give them."

"I never tried much with pretty words, either," said Steven.

"If you can't do that," Sylvanus propounded, waving his
cheroot with an all-inclusive gesture, "give them presents.
Nothing makes a woman feel better than a present. Especially
doodads. Don't give them useful things. Get things with frills
on them, useless, silly ones. Then you've got them."

"Maybe," said Steven, "I can do that."

"Above all, don't make the mistake of being afraid of a
woman because she's a woman. There's nothing to be afraid of.
Treat them like a goose. That's what they are. Handle them
just the way you would a goose."

Steven wasn't sure if Sylvanus was proving helpful. He
questioned whether or not they were speaking of the same
thing at all. To clear this up he said, "What do you do if—I
mean, supposing you want to marry her?"

Sylvanus looked at him incredulously. He lay back on the
sand and looked up at the sky. He blew two smoke rings, send-

ing one inside the other. In a voice filled with wonder and patience, he said, "Then you can only ask somebody to feel sorry for you. Nobody can help you."

Steven asked nothing more. He wondered how he could still find likable such a scoundrel as Sylvanus.

Ten

ONCE AGAIN STEVEN was wrong about the beachcombers. Next day the boat was in place at both inlets, and he and Sylvanus crossed without being molested. Sylvanus appeared to lose interest in the combers, as if disappointed in them, and turned to study the land. He cared not at all for the intrinsic beauties of nature, but saw them only in terms of how they added to real-estate values. His plans became more grandiose with every step they took.

They were caught unawares a mile after New River.

Abruptly, quickly, neatly, Theron and his two men sprang up from behind a hillock of sand piled by the tide. In their hands, lifted with the threat to strike, were stout lengths of jagged fatwood pine.

Silently, Steven raised his hands at the order. The clubs, he thought, weren't as bad as a pistol. He had feared a pistol. But they would stand a chance against the clubs.

Sylvanus followed suit in raising his hands. For the first time the boomer was entirely serious. His eyes went about. He seemed to be figuring something of his own.

The smallest of the men was left in front of them, with his

club raised. "You try to move," Theron threatened, "and he'll put one of you on the sand. We'll get the other from the back."

As Theron and the second man went around and behind him to open his haversack and take out the mail bag, Steven said, "That's United States mail. You won't find anything except trouble in there."

Theron hawed. "The kind of trouble in here is the kind I'm looking for." There was the sound of a knife slitting canvas. They began to shuffle the letters, examining and feeling of each envelope, tearing open the likely ones and ripping apart the newspapers.

That told Steven something. They knew Sylvanus was sending his money by mail, but they didn't know how.

Sylvanus's geniality returned. He began to talk. "Your method of robbing people is direct, but certainly old-fashioned." His shook his head with disapproval. "It rarely succeeds and you must pay for it in the end."

"You sound as if you know a better way," Theron told him.

"Oh, yes," Sylvanus replied. "Do it quietly, legally, and above all, pleasantly."

"We can be as pleasant as you want to be," Theron advised.

"But not as legal," Sylvanus pointed out. He turned his head. Steven caught his glance, saw him briefly nod and smile. At first Steven didn't know what he meant. Then he saw that Sylvanus indicated he would keep on talking, to perhaps divert the men's attention, giving them a chance for action.

Theron interrupted Sylvanus's lecture on the technique of robbery when he said of the mail bag, "Nothing here. I'll search the carrier," he told his companion. "You look through the passenger's suitcase while he goes on telling us how to do it."

Sylvanus continued to instruct them. But his comments had no effect. The sharp-edged club was held just as threateningly at them.

Tightly, trying to keep down his rising tide of fury and remain cool, Steven watched the suitcase yanked open and its contents of clothes flung about. He felt Theron's hands dipping into his haversack and taking out the articles there, which were dropped on the ground.

When the suitcase yielded nothing, Theron instructed, "Search the passenger."

As Sylvanus had his pockets explored he sighed and advised, "You're wasting your time. Hasn't it occurred to you yet that the money wasn't brought along?" He continued to scold them.

Now Theron's hands came around from in back of Steven. They began to go inside his clothes. He tensed, waiting a chance.

The small man holding the club stepped forward a little, so that he stood closer, to watch. Steven gauged the distance. If the man deviated his interest for an instant, he could reach him.

Theron's paw came around his side and yanked at the pocket of his shirt. Steven began to twist away, but the club came up on him. Theron grunted knowledge gleaned from Steven's movement, and pulled out the papers from the pocket.

Sylvanus, who had been speaking rapidly, now said slowly and coolly to the man in front of him, "Well, he's got the money. You can put up your club."

Involuntarily, the eyes of the little man were drawn away from his duty to the papers Theron had found. Steven's arm sped out on the second.

The club went high into the air and dropped to the sand with a slicking sound a dozen yards away. Steven faced the small man, but before he could reach for him, the man ran like a rabbit for the brush at the top of the beach.

Steven turned, to see Sylvanus rolling about on the sand with the second beachcomber, their legs and arms flailing. Theron, at Steven's action, had stuffed the papers in his pocket. Now he turned to help his companion with Sylvanus as Steven came back.

To meet him, Theron grabbed up his stick which had been put down on the sand. He swung it at Steven viciously. Putting up his arm to ward off the blow, Steven caught Theron's wrist. The stick came down, striking Steven on the side of the head and slipping out of Theron's grasp.

Steven snatched at the club and came up with it as Theron rushed him. He swung, and caught the bearded beachcomber on the upper arm. There was a sharp crack. Theron howled. His left arm dropped to his side, where it hung uselessly. It flapped there as he ran for the scrub.

Only then did Steven know how dazed he was from the blow he had received.

Theron had gained the undergrowth and disappeared before he could think to follow. He called to Sylvanus, heard him answer, became aware that the boomer was beside him, breathing heavily. It wasn't until then that Steven realized the second comber had also beat a hasty retreat.

There was no noise back in the scrub when they hurried to it. There were few marks where the men had passed, and soon they were to be seen no more. Steven and Sylvanus stared about. Steven saw how useless it would be to pursue them. The men knew their way back in the mazes of the thick trees and bushes that in a short way became swamp; he didn't. The only satisfaction he had was in knowing that he had hurt Theron. But Theron carried a greater one; he had the money envelope.

They made their way back to their strewn belongings on the beach. Steven made one search of his pocket in the hope that Theron had not taken all the papers. The pocket was empty.

"We seem," Sylvanus observed, "to have won the battle and lost the war." Sylvanus had a smudge across one cheek, but otherwise he was intact, almost unruffled. His bowler still clung to his head, and from beneath its rim his dark eyes carried enjoyment of the fight.

Steven caressed the side of his head. When Sylvanus inquired, solicitously, about it, Steven replied, "He'll remember what he got longer than I will." Gloomily he added, "But I'm counting on remembering how I was caught by them in the first place."

They bent to gather their belongings. "It's too bad about the money," Sylvanus said sympathetically. "I wouldn't have had it happen to you for the world, Steven. I never really expected it would."

Steven trembled a little with reaction from the fight and the thought of the money as he picked up the mail and put it back into the slit pouch. A thousand dollars was nearly two years of his pay as a mail carrier. He wasn't sure of what would happen about it. The government had to make good. Perhaps he would have to make good. The least was that he would lose his job.

Another thought struck him. He didn't carry money of his own with him, having no need for it. Sylvanus must. "Did they get your wallet?" he asked.

"Didn't you see?" Sylvanus asked. "My man had it in his fist after he went through me. I took it back from him while we had our arms around each other." He patted his pocket.

Not until that night could Steven think out clearly everything that had happened. Sylvanus, spent from the walking, lay like a dead man, without even taking off his hat, and snored.

Watching him, Steven reflected that his actions were peculiar. He didn't seem nearly as disturbed by the attack as he should have been. His cajolery during it was almost abnormal. Even though he expected to get his money back, he was too nonchalant about its theft

The wonder stole into Steven that perhaps Sylvanus had an agreement with the beachcombers, that it all had been fixed, and that the boomer would get most of his money back from them as well as being repaid by the government.

Yet he was unable to fathom how this could be, in what manner Sylvanus would trust the combers. And he had fought them. Yet, Steven reflected, he had caught only a glimpse of Sylvanus and the other man struggling. He hadn't seen the manner of their parting. There was little likelihood that his fighting had been pretense, put on as soon as the money was in the possession of the men. But Steven couldn't escape the fact that it could have been pretended.

He turned this over in his mind all the next day as they went along. The only time he stopped trying to work it out was when Sylvanus stumbled upon a paper nautilus. The white, fragile, serrated shell was one of the most perfect Steven had ever seen. He told Sylvanus, "I'd like to have that if you ain't got any special use for it."

"Oh, I have. A woman would appreciate a pretty like this. It's the kind of thing I was telling you about. I'll give it to the best-looking girl in Miami."

A jealous fright, greater than that of the loss of the money, entered Steven.

Sylvanus fell into the boat at Miami nearly in a state of collapse after the three days of carrying his suitcase along the beach. But he still had left spirit enough to smile when Steven told him, "You can pay your passage here."

"You expect me to pay you for losing my money, Steven?"

After all that had happened, and in his frustration at not being able to figure out things that bothered him, Steven felt savage. But he tried to keep his voice as pleasant as that of Sylvanus when he said, "That didn't have anything to do with the trip. You want to get across, or you want to stay here with the skeeters and hogs?"

Sylvanus laughed. "I was just joking."

He took out his wallet and gave Steven five dollars. Instinctively, Steven looked closely, but could see no one-hundred-dollar bills. He felt foolish at his act. He didn't understand how Sylvanus could possibly be in possession of his own money. Not when he had seen Theron stuff it in his pocket.

When they arrived at the freshwater spring in the middle of the bay, Sylvanus took advantage of the stop to put his personal appearance right. He straightened his clothes, brushing them, flattening them, and arranged his cravat. He opened his suitcase and took out his shaving materials.

Steven was willing to wait while Sylvanus scraped the beard from his face. He even drew water for him in the bailing bucket. Idly, Steven watched him.

Sylvanus didn't remove his hat while he shaved. The fact didn't impress Steven at first. Then it did.

A sting of realization went through him. He remembered how Sylvanus had kept the bowler continually clamped to his head.

Steven was so sure of his suspicion that he didn't question it at all.

Moving quickly, he reached for the bowler and lifted it off before Sylvanus could object or protect it. Steven turned it upside down. There, inside the high crown of the bowler, was the money envelope. He took it out, and saw that what held it in place was a flattened ball of pine pitch.

Sylvanus laughed again, lightly, easily. He kept on shaving, casually and unperturbed, as he said, "I was going to tell you as soon as we landed, Steven. You see, I didn't think your pocket was the safest place. I took it out while you were asleep the first night we were on the beach. Don't you think it worked out to be a good idea?"

Steven marveled that the man could face him blandly, without a tremor in his voice or a hint of guilt in his look. "First-rate," he replied, "except for me not knowing about it."

Sylvanus bent to look into his mirror, which he had set up on a thwart. He shaved his chin. "I thought it best for you not to know," he explained. "Then you wouldn't give it away. And I didn't say anything later in case they came at us again."

Steven had it all, then. Sylvanus's fighting had been real. The boomer had no agreement with the beachcombers, but worked on his own. His clever waiting, before distracting the man holding the club, until the first instant Theron had the papers in his hand, was a calculated plan. That way there was no opportunity for either Theron or Steven himself to learn that the money was not among the papers.

Steven took enjoyment at the thought of Theron's surprise

when he examined the papers. He almost admired the rascality of Sylvanus. He told him, "I don't know whether to cut you up for shark-bait now, or wait until some is needed."

Sylvanus wiped his face dry of shaving soap. "Why, Steven," he expostulated, "you can't say I didn't save the money for you? You can't tell anyone that? Of course not."

Steven reflected that he couldn't. He saw how it would look if he told the true story. It would seem that the money hadn't been handled properly and Sylvanus had to do it himself. The man had him there. He was cute, very cute.

Sylvanus seemed to read his thoughts. His eyes danced with merriment when he held out his hand for the money envelope, suggesting, "I'll take it now."

"You get it after you identify yourself to the postmaster."

As he took up his rowing again, Steven decided that no authority would do anything about the tampering with the mail either on the part of Sylvanus or Theron and the beach-combers. Sylvanus had created a tight position for himself and in any case would tell a better story than Steven. Oat McCarty, the present sheriff of the county, wouldn't move an inch out of Miami to try to catch the beachcombers. And no one would blame him for his chicken-heartedness, for everyone knew they couldn't be found back in the Everglades. Even the government wouldn't send an investigator this far, especially when the result had been no actual theft.

Sylvanus, when he first saw Miami, recoiled in horror.

"Is *that* the city? God Almighty," he whispered. Then he brightened. "However, the worse it is, the better it can be made."

Freshly groomed and rested, the boomer went ahead of Steven up the dock in front of the trading post. Steven stopped on the shore, for this time Charming Tiger was here among the encamped Seminoles. More than ever now did Steven want to get the Indian to tell him what he might know of the combers.

In this he was disappointed. Charming Tiger was in no condition to be interviewed. A great hulk of a man, overflowing with flesh, he sat on the ground in his leggings with his white man's shirt hanging out. There was nothing unusual in this, but there was something definitely wrong in the sight of his turban being awry, and his eyes being glazed and bloodshot.

On the ground in front of the massive Indian was lined up an assortment of whisky bottles and cans of brandied peaches and cherries, some of them opened and their contents consumed, others yet to be investigated. About him were his two squaws, both clad in vermilion from a single bolt of goods Charming Tiger had once traded at the store. Unable to move their man, they were building a palmetto shelter over him. They laughed and giggled happily as they worked.

To Steven's address Charming Tiger could only gurgle, "Wy-oh-mey." He pointed to a whisky bottle and repeated, "Wy-oh-mey."

Steven gave up. He looked toward the store.

Adie stood there. His heart leaped and then steadied to a dull thump. Sylvanus Hurley was with her. He was giving her the paper nautilus, bowing gracefully. She was staring at him and taking it.

Eleven

BY THE TIME STEVEN reached the trading post, Sylvanus was inside. He had introduced himself all around to those gathering for their mail, and launched his campaign to the assemblage.

"Do you know what they say upstate about your fair city?" he demanded. "They say there's nothing here except insects, vermin, mud, malaria, Indians, desolation, and abomination. They say there is discomfort, disease, death, and poverty. Nothing, they tell the world, will grow here but coontie and mangroves, and nobody decent lives here and nobody decent wants to."

There were murmurs of surprise, indignation, and resentment. Steven caught Adie's glance from across the room. He felt better when he saw her eyes widen and her smile, but he didn't like the sight of the shell in her hands.

"They not only tell you such things," Sylvanus went on, "they print them. Right out in a circular. I've got one here and I want you to look at it." He took a printed flimsy from his pocket and handed it to a burly, popeyed man who leaned against the counter as if needing the support to hold him up. "You read it first, Sheriff," Sylvanus told Oat McCarty.

Oat stared at it, his face getting purple with rage. "Why," he exclaimed, "this here is all lies and libel! The man who wrote this ought to be hung!"

"Certainly he should," Sylvanus agreed quickly. He took the circular from Oat's hand and gave it to Dan Bunnell, who had been craning for a look. It was passed among the people as Sylvanus went on, including new arrivals in his remarks.

"You know, and I know, that's the work of paper-town sharks who want people to stay in their towns. They're just trying to run down the truth about a place they know in their black hearts is better than their own. I expect you realize what I mean by that. I mean this magnificent city of Miami and the incomparable climate you have here. I mean," Sylvanus continued, warming up and speaking as though quoting from something he had read, "the resounding fact that here there are two hundred and forty sunny days in the year, while the cities of Europe have only sixty-four."

Steven glanced around. No one had paid any attention to the arrival of the mail. He unslung his haversack and pulled out the mail bag, putting it on the counter in front of Bunnell.

The trader didn't take any notice of it. Steven had wondered how he would explain the slit in the bag. Now he wouldn't have to right away.

Bunnell stood open-mouthed, lost in the newcomer's words. His hawk-faced maiden sisters had come in to fasten their pale eyes on Sylvanus with repressed admiration. The several dozen people listened to Sylvanus.

"There can be no question," he announced in his most charming manner, "as to this section's desirability as a winter resort. It is greatly superior to any you can find in the entire world. From personal experience I can tell you that includes France, Italy, and even far-famed Egypt."

A single questioning voice spoke up. Steven was glad to see that it came from Adie's father, who asked, "How do we know you are not a paper-town shark yourself? How do we know you have not come here to boom our city to false values?"

The crowd turned from Titus to Sylvanus for his answer. He had it on the tip of his tongue instantly. "Perhaps I am exactly what you say, sir. But perhaps that is precisely what Miami needs. 'Fire to fight fire,'" he quoted. "As for false values, there can be none here. No top value can be placed upon your unrivaled attributes, which need only to be developed and placed before the world to make this the garden spot of the universe."

The faces expressed satisfaction with this frank and flattering reply. Titus looked thoughtful. All continued to listen raptly.

"I'm here to help you," Sylvanus preached. "I don't say I won't perhaps be helping myself a little at the same time, for that would be a palpable lie, and I do not lie. Together we can make Miami the envy of the nation. Here will come statesmen, leaders, the arts and the professions, the rich and the cultured. A great city will rise before us, and it will be of our own making. And the way to do this is to raise a crop more profitable than any other. Here, we will sell climate, and in it we shall raise sick Yankees and investors. . . ."

Steven had to admire Sylvanus. He hadn't been half an hour in the town and he was calling it "ours." A Yankee himself, he was referring to Yankees as a source of revenue which could be raised like sugar cane.

His gift of gab already had the people stupefied, won, and hopeful of his presence for a new future. He came like the harbinger of a spring never seen here in the continuous summer. Most of all, he was a good show. He could hold listeners, and an audience acted upon him like a challenge to be met and overcome.

People crowded around him. Finally, Steven had the chance to seek out Adie. Looking at the nautilus in her hand he said, "I didn't keep my promise so good, but I'll do my best to find you a bigger one." Her presence was as he had known it would be. It was heady, like wine to which he had yet to get accustomed.

She made no reference to Sylvanus. "How are the morning glories?" she asked. "And the possum and the flamingoes and the gopher?"

She remembered. She had admired them as being the best things among which to live.

Steven murmured that he hadn't stopped by at Hypoluxo on this trip. His eyes went to Sylvanus as he spoke, as if to indicate that he was the reason. Steven wanted to tell Adie about him at once, reveal the man to her before Sylvanus had any chance to present himself as a worthy individual. But Adie had not mentioned Sylvanus. Steven wished she had. By her omission Sylvanus was between them as if she had shouted it.

"Will you come for supper with us tonight?" she asked. "And really come?"

Readily in his wish, almost eagerly in his expression of it, Steven accepted.

Bunnell gave Sylvanus the room next to the one Steven occupied. As Steven spruced himself to go to the Tituses, he could hear them talking through the thin partition. Sylvanus pumped the trader for information, adroitly asking questions, persuasively getting Bunnell's agreement to his proposals. Steven had never before heard the fat trader so enthusiastic.

"What we have here," Sylvanus told him, "is a city divided against itself. Part of it is across the river, part of it is here. The first thing to be done is to join them."

"How are you going to do that?"

"By operating a ferry service," Sylvanus explained. "All that's needed is a rope across run through a couple of rings on a light barge. The charges, I should say, would be ten cents a person, a quarter for a passenger vehicle, and fifty cents for a loaded vehicle."

"That's pretty stiff," Bunnell began, "and there ain't any vehicles—"

"There will be," Sylvanus asserted. "I thought perhaps the city might be willing to issue to me the franchise for this in exchange for the service the ferry would render."

"Hell and damnation," the trader told him, "you don't need no franchise. You just go ahead and start the ferry."

"I like to do things properly."

Bunnell appeared then to realize more fully the opportunities in the idea and the manner in which Sylvanus planned to take advantage of them. In a knowing tone, he said, "You mean in case somebody later on gave you competition with another ferry, then you'd have the exclusive right?"

"One," said Sylvanus, "must look to the future."

"You bet," Bunnell agreed. "And in such case, I think I can fix it so you get a paper reading right. I ain't only for my health Chairman of the Board of County Commissioners, which is about all the government the town has got, too. The only thing," the trader went on, "is that maybe such a paper would be worth something. I don't say it would be worth a half interest in the ferry, but with some capital thrown in, too, a company might be formed."

Sylvanus chuckled. Their voices dropped to a whisper. After a few moments they left the room, still talking in low tones.

Bunnell was alone in the store when Steven started out for

the Titus house. The trader didn't mention the slit mail bag, and Steven didn't bring it up. Steven told himself it was not because of Adie, but for protection of the Miami people, including the trader himself, that he gave the warning about Sylvanus.

"Maybe he'll do some good here," he told Bunnell, "but he'll get the best of it for himself."

Bunnell looked up, scowling. "Steven, if you heard anything about the ferry, you keep it to yourself."

"That don't matter," Steven said. "That's the least part of it."

"Well, we don't want anybody else hearing about it. Anything about it," he stipulated.

"I'm not saying anything about that. That's only—"

"It's the start of big things here. I believe this man's coming is going to be the best thing that ever happened to the section. New, pushing kind of blood is what's needed. You heard him talk, and he's got it."

"I spent three days on the beach with him," Steven pointed out. "I got to know something about him. More'n you know right now, but maybe not as much as you'll learn later if you ain't careful and don't go slow."

The trader adopted a patronizing attitude, speaking to Steven as to a young boy who did not see the larger matters of life in their true light. "We'll get along, Stevie. We can take care of ourselves. You just carry your mail and don't go to worrying about things in this end of the county."

Steven saw it was useless to speak to Bunnell. Led by Sylvanus, the trader was one of a kind with him, perhaps not as sharp, but sharp enough to appreciate the other's tricks and be a part of them. Steven wondered if the other people could be told. He remembered the looks on their faces when they listened to Sylvanus. Suddenly he understood that they couldn't be convinced. Mesmerized by Sylvanus, their eyes were closed.

He decided to follow Bunnell's advice. That is, with everyone except Adie. He could tell her. He felt sure he could.

Jealousy jolted into him again when he arrived at the Tituses and found Sylvanus there. What was more, Sylvanus had brought Adie a bouquet of flowers.

She was arranging them in a vase, and thanking him. When she touched the fragrant cluster of oleanders she seemed to caress them. Steven wondered where the man obtained them, remembered the bush on the way along the path. It was as simple as that.

Sylvanus greeted him affably, though in his eyes there was a delighted, mocking glint to comment on the fact that after giving Steven advice on romantic affairs, they were now courting the same girl. At first Steven didn't understand how Sylvanus could be asked here at all and so soon. His heart sank at the initial conviction that Adie had asked him. To his relief, Mr. Titus's remarks made it evident that it was he who had asked the man. Titus wanted to discuss with him his ideas on developing Miami.

They sat down to dinner, the frail Mrs. Titus with a shawl about her shoulders at one side of the square table, and her husband opposite her. Steven was heartened that he sat with Adie on a third side, while Sylvanus occupied the fourth alone. It was Adie who prepared and served the meal, bringing in a tremendous savory roast of venison.

To Steven each bite was like a holy thing. But it was Sylvanus who praised its excellence. To Mrs. Titus he said, "You not only have a beautiful daughter, but a jewel in the kitchen as well." Sylvanus held a piece of meat on his fork before plopping it into his mouth. "This is nectar of the gods."

Stephen could not see Adie's face, nor did he bring himself to look to find out how she took the extravagant compliments Sylvanus showered upon her. He consoled himself with the knowledge that Sylvanus by his own declaration was not sincere, and that Adie would sense this.

At the same time he felt himself to be at a disadvantage. The other man's words flowed from him in smooth, often flowery, cadences. Steven was not practiced in such talk, and could say little. He had not much chance, for Sylvanus dominated the conversation. Steven even felt shabby in his drilling cloth while his rival sat there in comparative finery.

A surge of new resentment went through him when Sylvanus, after glancing at him, began to tell the story of the beachcombers and his money. It had been Steven's understanding that neither of them was to say anything about this. Now he saw that Sylvanus had put him, alone, in the position of not mentioning it. Because the man wanted to establish Steven in a bad light with the Tituses, or because he wanted to be sure Steven would not present only his side of it, he was protecting himself.

Sylvanus told it as a joke, as an amusing incident. He didn't run Steven down for not caring better for his money, but it had the same effect. Adie glanced once at Steven when the part about the beachcombers was related, then attended Sylvanus again.

Steven let him finish. Then, trying to keep his voice steady, trying not to take it too seriously yet at the same time make himself plain, he said, "It looked to me he was meaning to make a thousand dollars extra out of the trick."

Sylvanus didn't need to lead the laughter which followed. Mrs. Titus, her eyes unnaturally bright from her illness, seemed to penetrate the rivalry between the young men. It added to her not taking Steven's remark literally. She laughed. Adie and her father, their faces beaming at the sound from her, followed suit.

Steven decided he had been too jocular. In his care not to sound outright accusing, he had overdone it. Mrs. Titus's amusement had clinched this. Uncontrollable fury rode him at Sylvanus getting off so easily. He said darkly, "Well, that's what he was doing."

"Of course I was," Sylvanus agreed, chuckling. "Only you were too smart for me."

Titus pushed back his chair and rose, slapping Steven on the back. The gesture was meant to appease him about an accusation that was too fantastic to have any basis of truth.

They left the table, and Titus said to Sylvanus, "I'm not at all sure that your ideas of cutting up the land in lots for tourists is sound. It still seems to me farming and working the land productively is the thing."

"Both," answered Sylvanus. "The shore front and a little back is for the tourists and investors. Back of that you can work the ground. But selling the sun instead of tomatoes is the real thing. Because we've got something to sell that can't be found anywhere else."

The discussion of tourists and farming lasted through most of the evening. Adie listened silently, turning her eyes from one to the other of the men as they spoke. Steven entered the talk but little, saying once that maybe years from now what Sylvanus proposed could be done, but it was too soon to think about it.

"Nothing is too soon to think about," Titus disagreed. "I question only the manner of its application at this time." He glanced at Sylvanus, still evaluating him.

Mrs. Titus struggled up from her chair, excusing herself, and Adie hurried to her. She accompanied her mother into the other room of the house.

When the men resumed their chairs again, Sylvanus defended himself. Out and out he called himself a parasite. "I'll do nothing for the land itself. Except create a demand for it and," he said impressively to Titus, "perhaps raise the value of your homestead to ten, twenty times what it's worth now."

"I'm getting along all right as it is," Titus argued, "without risking what I have in a land boom."

Steven cheered this refusal to accept Sylvanus immediately. "Folks don't need or want more than they got now," he said.

Sylvanus ignored him. He spoke to Titus. "Wasn't that a coontie mill I saw in your yard when I arrived this evening? And don't I understand, sir, that coontie is a wild plant that can't be cultivated profitably? When that runs out, you'll need something else. And you've got it: land, Mr. Titus, land for tourists, for sick people who want to get well, for the rich who can afford to get away from the northern winter. And that takes a pusher, an evil, wicked, stealing pusher like myself."

Titus, though chuckling at Sylvanus's description of himself, remained only half-convinced. When Adie reappeared, it was time for the guests to leave, and Sylvanus continued the argument over her hand when he took it to say goodbye. Addressing Titus rather than Adie, he proposed:

"You'll see it, Mr. Titus, you will. I wouldn't want to be on the outs with the father of such an exquisite creature as you have here." He said this while looking straight into Adie's face, and now he spoke to her directly. "And upon whose loveliness I hope to look again if I may be permitted to call?"

Steven held his breath to note how Adie took this. All evening he had tried to determine what she thought of Sylvanus. She had laughed over many things he said. She treated him, when he was serious, with courtesy and interest. Little other indication had come from her. Now she moved in the barest hint of a curtsy, saying, "We are always here."

Sylvanus went with Titus out to the porch. Steven, remaining behind, wasn't sure if Adie saw through his rival. He remembered what Sylvanus had said about women. At the thought of Sylvanus being here throughout the week with Adie, while he would come but once, he wanted to warn her. Nodding in the direction of the porch, he told her, "I never saw a man who could give lies with such a straight face. He don't mean a thing he says."

"Doesn't he, Steven?" By the tone of her voice, Steven realized, sharply, that he had said the wrong thing. Amused more than offended, Adie went on, "That isn't very complimentary to me."

Hastily, he apologized, stumbling over his words. "It wasn't anything like that I meant."

"What did you mean?" Again she was laughing at him, and again it confused him.

"It's just I can't make speeches like him." The threat of

Sylvanus stirred him to boldness. "But anything I say to you—well, what I say is something I mean."

"I'll remember that, Steven."

In turn he remembered her reply, and the way she looked when she made it. The single thing he didn't like about it was that he made her solemn while Sylvanus made her gay.

$\mathcal{T}welve$

THE SUN WAS LIGHTING with pink the ragged line of tiny islands in the bay when Steven ate his grits in the kitchen of the trading post. Faintly he heard the voices of Sylvanus and Bunnell in the store. Emily, the eldest of the trader's sisters, served him, while Clara sat sewing the slit in the mail bag. The old maids were nearly alike in being lean, tight-lipped, and having noses so large that they were virtually beaks.

This morning they were excited. They were voluble and friendly to Steven, but the comments they made were their own strong opinions in which they took a pleasure, their advice to him oblique.

Steven was startled when Clara said, "He's a handsome one, as handsome as ever I seen."

"He's bad," Emily announced, "bad to the bone." Her words were ones of denunciation, but her tone was of praise, as though she couldn't keep from her voice some secret that overpowered her.

"We know he tried to steal the money on you," Clara told Steven.

"It's the kind of thing a man like him does," Emily said. She was almost enthusiastic.

"But you won't get anybody else hereabouts to believe it," Clara finished. "He's got too much oil on his tongue. He'll make the truth slide off."

"It's already slid off," said Steven. It was plain that Sylvanus or Bunnell, or both, had spoken to the sisters. Their talk disturbed him further because he couldn't understand it. If they saw Sylvanus in his true light, they should be holding him in contempt. But their attitude was nearly one of worship.

"He's the kind who likes to do things around the corner instead of straight out," Emily said.

"He would rather sharp you instead of doing it fair even when he can do it fair," Clara observed.

A gleam, hungry and burning, came to Emily's faded eyes. "No woman should ever have anything to do with him. No woman should ever look at him." She spoke so vehemently that for a moment it brought silence to the kitchen.

Steven frankly stared. He had never seen Emily like this before. Both the sisters seemed moved by a strange passion they could not hold in check. Partial comprehension came to him when Clara explained:

"Emily's saying that because once, in the North before we come here, she had a beau. He looked almost like this one. It almost could be him. Most of all, he acted like him. He had the same kind of soul."

"You don't call it a soul," her sister corrected.

"It was about it that Emily had the falling out with him," Clara continued. "They was to be married, with the date set, the things bought, even the dress. Then she blessed him out to a finish because he wouldn't promise to mend his ways."

Emily made it clear, "I never cared which nor whether about the whole matter."

Steven saw how much she cared, how it had ridden her life and that of her sister. And now, to have here, in Sylvanus, a duplicate of the man Emily had loved, stirred and moved them both curiously.

Clara sewed rapidly on the mail bag. She put in the last stitches. She bent her head, chewed on the tough carpet thread, broke it, and muttered, "He wasn't worth the salt you can put on a dime. The same as this one."

Emily whirled on Steven, her eyes blazing. "You'll have to go some to beat him!" she cried. "You'll have to go faster than you can go! He'll best you every time. He'll do things you never thought about. He'll get her and you won't. If you ain't careful you'll lose out. Even if you're careful, you'll lose!"

Steven rose from his half-finished breakfast. Emily sounded crazy. She wasn't hoping he would get Adie instead of Sylvanus. She was hoping Sylvanus would get her. As the man before had not married her, she wished, vicariously for herself, the present duplicate to succeed with another.

He left the kitchen and went to his room to pack his haversack.

The mail bag was filled and ready when Steven went into the store. He eyed the half-dozen large unshucked coconuts placed beside it on the counter. The stems were tied together with heavy fishline. On the dry brown husk of each, printed in bold letters with an indelible blue pencil, was the address: " 'Dr.' Bethune, Palm Beach, Florida."

Both Sylvanus and the trader glanced slyly at Steven. When Steven said nothing, Sylvanus observed, "You got a little extra mail this morning."

"Maybe they'll serve," Bunnell said, "to show the folks up at your end of the county what cocos look like."

Steven decided to take the joke in fair spirit, and to carry it through. It would be no joke carrying the heavy nuts all the way. But by doing so he could throw back in their faces the attempt to devil him. "We use this size for inch-scale samples of the real thing," he said. Peering at them, he went on, "I don't see any name telling who they're from."

"That's information," Sylvanus said quickly, "the postmaster can't give out, even to the carrier."

His statement fell rather flat. Already Steven had taken some of the wind out of their sails. The trader, in his position as postmaster, tried not to look ashamed of himself. His lips pouted and he appeared willing, if it were not for Sylvanus, to call the whole thing off. "I don't say," he told Steven, "you can't dump them when you're out of sight and pick others for delivery when you get to the lake."

"They got stamps on them," Steven pointed out. "They're regular mail. You know I can't do anything like that." His tone chided Bunnell for even suggesting such a thing.

He took up the mail and slung the coconuts over his shoulder so that they hung like his shoes on the other shoulder. He turned to Sylvanus. He didn't care if Bunnell heard what he had to say; he wanted him to hear it. To Sylvanus he advised, "There's one thing I didn't get around to telling you."

"What's that?"

"You touch a hair on her head, then you got me to deal with."

"Steven," Sylvanus protested, "why do you always think the worst of me?"

"Because I know what's in you," Steven replied evenly. "I saw it. Maybe you didn't think I was looking, but I was."

Bunnell, siding with the newcomer, told Steven, "We don't want any threats—"

Sylvanus motioned him to silence. He asked Steven, "What makes you think Miss Titus is the kind that can be harmed?"

"She ain't. It's only because you'll try that I'm saying it."

The more serious Steven became, the more genial Sylvanus showed himself to be. "How do you know I won't be honorable about her?"

"You said in your own words that ain't a part of you."

Sylvanus spoke surprisingly. "Sometimes men lie to themselves. And sometimes they change."

"You got a powerful way to go."

Sylvanus looked thoughtful. "With Miss Titus," he said, "I wonder."

Steven contemplated this remark as he went out. He didn't accept it. If Sylvanus meant what he said, it would be the worst thing that could happen. Then Adie might believe him. Steven didn't even want to consider that.

At the river shore he strode to the shelter built over Charming Tiger. Last night the Indian's celebration still lasted. This morning he lay with his squaws on either side of him for warmth. Tiger snored with great, stentorian snorts.

Steven bent and took him by the shoulder and shook. Charming Tiger's bulk jiggled, but his eyes remained closed. Steven shook harder. The squaws opened their eyes sleepily and sat up, but their man was not to be awakened. Giving up, Steven addressed the women. "Me Pierton—mail carrier—want see Tiger—soon."

They didn't understand. One of them said, "Me Seminole, good. Ojus, me good too much, umcah."

Steven tried again, using what Seminole he knew. He made gestures. Pointing to Tiger, he indicated sickness. They thought he meant Tiger's present condition and readily agreed, showing expanses of white teeth. Steven pointed north and told them of a former sickness. He had found Tiger really ill and taken him to Doc, who brought him around.

The squaws then comprehended who he was. With motions, Steven elaborated the message they were to give to Tiger. This time they grasped it. Nodding their heads vigorously and pointing at Steven, they repeated his admonition, "Soon come see me."

Walking the beach now, walking away from Adie, leaving her behind with Sylvanus, Steven took little pleasure in what before had been delightful sights. Every step he took was a danger. From this time on the trip down was to be merely a race to get to Adie, and the trip back another frenzied hurry so that he could start south again.

Each yard he covered was a torture of wondering what Adie and Sylvanus were doing together. The wash of the ocean seemed to bring him the notes of the way they must be enjoying each other's company. Sometimes he fancied they were laughing at him.

Along the whole way he searched for a nautilus. It was to be larger, more perfect, than the one Sylvanus had stumbled upon. He found a number, and several he was sure were equal prizes to bring Adie. Over one he hesitated, thinking it bested that of Sylvanus. But he couldn't be sure, and regretfully discarded it. He wanted there to be no doubt it overshadowed that of his rival.

Stubbornly, he carried the coconuts. They were lead weights, unwieldy, banging against each other as he walked. The line fastening them together cut into his shoulder. He told himself it was mail and he was required to carry it. He had said he would do it, and he was doing it. But these weren't the only reasons; there was something else, contained in a blind, perverse hate which seemed to make him want to punish himself. It was like the feelings of the Bunnell sisters, as if some of that had transmuted itself to him.

Eighteen miles below Palm Beach, Steven was surprised to see a schooner standing a short distance offshore. There was activity on the beach. A small lighter was being operated between the boat and the shore. As he drew closer he saw piles of lumber, kegs of nails, and other building materials. The lighter was just pulling out again as he came up. He halloed the men in it, and they rested their oars.

"We're the government!" they shouted to his question. "Going to build one of the houses of refuge here."

So they were getting at it. "About time!" he called back.

"We work slow, being the government," one of the men advised. "But we work good."

"You better," Steven said, "or a blow'll take it."

"You wait till you see it."

Another man in the lighter spoke up. "If you're the carrier

along here, your uncle Jim has got some of the work transporting. You'll be seeing him for a spell, and farther down at the other sites."

They rowed out, laboriously, to the schooner.

Steven glanced at the site here, and approved it. Back of the ridge stood a scraggly orange grove, gone sour after its owner abandoned it years ago. It could be brought back, and would give the keeper and wrecked sailors fruit. He examined the heavy oak timbers that had already been piled far above tidemark. He had never seen such fine, clean-grained lumber.

It excited Steven that Cap Jim had some of the work. And Jesse would want to know; Steven remembered Jesse's desire to get the job at one of the stations, and looked forward to having him on his route.

Jesse already knew about it. At the store he greeted Steven with a whoop, yelling that he'd be moving soon. "I got the job practically in my pocket. Ain't it a caution with the government—putting things off for years and then all of a sudden doing them?"

Cap Jim and Gerald were there. Cap explained that the reason he had been hired was that he could put his flat-bottomed sharpie right up on the beach to unload materials. Gerald told Steven, referring to Adie, "You wouldn't 'ave my word abawt that there boy, an' now look wot you gone an' got yourself into."

"That ain't your business, you damned Conch!" Cap Jim roared. He sent Gerald, who didn't appear to mind, away with a kick. Cap Jim spread his beard into a wide grin at Steven. "It's my business. When's the wedding?"

Steven told him, "I never heard of any wedding."

"Grab her," advised Cap Jim. "Grab her quick if you want her. She'll like you all the more for it."

"Like I did Della," said Jesse. "Two days in Key West and then the preacher spoke words over us letting us do what we wanted from the first minute we set eyes on each other."

"It didn't work until now," Cap Jim taunted. "And maybe it ain't worked yet even after all you say."

Jesse inflated his round chest, crowing happily, "Della's caught, she's caught good and it'll be a boy."

Doc asked Steven, "What're you carrying them cocos for?"

Steven unslung and put them down. "They're mail," he said. "For you."

Doc peered at them over his spectacles. He snapped his armbands and exclaimed, "I never heard of such a thing! I never did!"

Steven explained it, starting at the beginning of his entire trip.

Cap Jim boomed, "You want anybody's neck wrung down there at Miami, or along the line, I'll—"

"I can do my own wringing," Steven told him, "if need be."

"But what'd you carry them cocos for, Stevie?" Jesse wanted to know. "If it'd been me, I wouldn't have moved a foot with them, stamps or no stamps. I can't figure out you lugging them all the way."

"I don't rightly know," said Steven, "myself. Except I brung them."

Thirteen

THE FERRY ACROSS THE MIAMI RIVER began operating in May. The barge, constructed by a boat-builder at Coconut Grove, was pulled across on its rope by the only Negro in the vicinity. Abaco was a huge Bahaman with yellow eyes and sprawling shoulders strong enough to pull the ferry against the flow of the stream at ebb tide.

Abaco and his craft were viewed with admiration and pride. Sylvanus was looked upon as having taken a first concrete step in carrying out his promises for the city. The two sections of the community were now connected by a formal means of transportation. It brought the county courthouse more into the city, and brought also the residents living north of the river into easier contact with the rest.

The ferry inspired several families who operated coontie mills to import light wagons and mules from Key West. Coontie was getting progressively more difficult to find on the south side of the river, and now people went afield for it, crossing over into new land.

Titus was among those to get a vehicle. He, with the others, grumbled at the price to be paid for transporting a load across the stream. But all were glad enough to have the service. No one protested the franchise given to Sylvanus and his company. Few, indeed, saw any significance in it and were only vaguely aware that a company of some kind had been formed.

Adie's father did not join those who went in with Sylvanus on offering property for sale at prices jumped so high that it took most people's breath away. Titus remained undecided, though Sylvanus was still working on him. Others staked off parts of their homesteads into lots. Bunnell, who owned a large tract on the point of the river, and Sylvanus, who acquired land of his own, went in together. From contributions of all interested parties advertisements, written by Sylvanus, were placed in northern newspapers.

A trickle of people, large enough for Sylvanus to claim it a good start, began to appear. Most of them came by the steamer route to Key West and back again. Some traveled on the itinerant schooners plying the coast. A few became Steven's foot-passengers along the beach. Ironically, he took their fares, brought to him by the efforts of Sylvanus.

Some people were disappointed in Miami and angry at what

they found. Others came to look, or spend a few weeks, and go away again. A fair number, though shocked at the prices asked, bought property for investment, or stayed. Interest, definite and promising, was being taken in the city.

In the other end of the county even greater changes were being prepared. Surveyors appeared for the construction of the narrow-gauge railway to run south for eight miles from Jupiter to the head of Lake Worth, crossing the land between Hobe Sound and the lake. Using Jupiter as the inspiration, three other stations, both mythological and mythical, were planned, to be called Mars, Venus, and Juno. Already it was dubbed "The Celestial Railroad."

Steamers were now running from Titusville, the northern terminus of the regular railroad from the north, to Indian River, more than halfway to the growing settlement at the Jupiter lighthouse. When the narrow-gauge was built they would run all the way. The plan became definite for a naphtha launch to be brought to the lake, to run between Juno and Palm Beach.

When Steven imparted this information to Jesse at the house of refuge, Jesse said he'd gotten out just in time. "I feel sorry, though," he said, "for that fellow Quimby who took my route from Jupiter. He'll lose his job. I taught him the walking good, too."

The first house of refuge along the beach was finished and Jesse had obtained the job as keeper. Because of the grove in back of the site, it was called the Orange Grove Station. It gave the Pagets the best shelter they had ever lived in.

Built solidly, it had a screened veranda all around and a high, sloping roof, said to be hurricane-proof. Inside, on the ground floor, were four rooms filled with manufactured furniture. A large loft above contained twenty iron cots with mattresses, bedding, and a supply of clothing. Here also were stored provisions, salt pork and beef, hardtack, and other food contained in sealed packages to be used only for the relief of shipwrecked mariners.

The work for Jesse was easy. Outside of a wreck, all he had to do was to put the tide gauge on record every day, note what vessels passed, and make a monthly report. Jesse had more trouble with his mother than he did with his duties. Linda, though she had the comfort of having her shoofly chair placed on the front veranda where no insects came in, was more caustic than ever. She didn't approve of the change. She didn't approve of anything. Mostly she still refused to accept Della amicably. Her resentment became nearly a hate, stemming from her daughter-in-law's promise to present her son with a child.

Della herself was happy. Of the house she said, "I don't know yet what to do with all the room."

"You give us about six years," Jesse told her, "and you won't have enough room to put all the people."

Steven now stopped overnight with the Pagets on his trips, sleeping in the loft. It made the second day's journey a little longer, but he didn't mind that in exchange for the company. With them he ate alligator tail, shredded palmetto bud, and baked coconut filled with sour orange juice. On his first stop with them Linda demanded, "What you doin' with yore sweetheart? You got land. What you waitin' on?"

"Maybe," said Steven, "for her to say something about it."

"Her? You're the one to say. I bet you never ast her yet."

Linda's accusation was more than true. He could tell Adie that what he might say to her he meant, but he could find little to say. Rather, he found a good many things, but could express few of them. Prepared, even rehearsed, they wouldn't come out in her presence. They didn't seem right at all. And somehow he could never make up new ones on the spur of the moment.

His urge, strange and new to him, terrible and wonderful, found him utterly lacking in preparation. Without Sylvanus, it would have been difficult enough. With him, it was doubly hard. Sylvanus was always there between them, often actually

there when he took the trouble to call on Adie the only evening of each week Steven could be with her.

Steven didn't see her every time he was in Miami, or often
for only snatches. The care of her mother sometimes interfered. Then he would have a longer period before looking
into her face to see how much of Sylvanus he could read there.
That she was attracted to Sylvanus was plain. How much was
not at all clear.

And Adie, instead of being helpful about this, or making
the way easier for Steven, seemed to enjoy the situation. She
didn't dangle her admirers one before the other, but she was
not averse to having two of them. And if, occasionally, there
was annoyance for Sylvanus talking too much, there was the
same for Steven talking too little. Perhaps what she wanted
was a man with attributes in between.

Waiting for her to learn that Sylvanus was not sincere failed
to succeed. She never showed enough displeasure with him
to indicate that she had discovered this. That she must, in time,
Steven was sure. But meanwhile his agony continued. To end
it, several times Steven decided to declare himself and have it
over with. But the thought of her not accepting him shut the
words in his throat. Once he tried to utter them, after Gerald,
surprisingly, gave him a present for her. Abruptly, the little
Conch said to him, "Wot you need to 'ave for 'er is some
thing of a trifle, good to look at. You tell 'er to put this 'ere in
'er 'air."

He had proffered a flower, blue, exquisite, and dainty, con-
trived out of tinted fish scales. Its manner of making he had
learned in his islands, and when Steven thanked him, he
scowled.

This he presented to Adie. He had never seen her so pleased,
not even at the possum hanging upside down in the tree
munching a persimmon. She put it in her hair without his
direction, where it glowed a deeper blue against the copper,
and told him, "Oh, Steven, it's the most beautiful thing I've
ever had."

The warmth of her appreciation affected him so encouragingly that he had begun to say all he wanted to tell her. "Miss Adie—"

"Steven!" she chided. "You've been calling me Adie."

"That's right. Well, Miss Adie, I . . ."

That was as far as he got. The realization that, automatically, he still addressed her formally, made him see how far away from her he was. It closed in over his thoughts, shutting them off. And when she had not been amused, but merely sober, he tried to figure out if this was a good or a bad sign, and could arrive at no conclusion.

He went to Hypoluxo to think about her, and remember the day she sat here as a boy and the things he said to her then. He said them over again. Always she seemed to fit them exactly. But it was no new thing to know that he had found what he wanted. He had seen that during the days they were on the beach together.

Once he pushed open the mahogany door of the house on the island and sensed, before he saw him, that there was someone else in the room. Charming Tiger sat motionless in one of the barrel chairs, overflowing it as though filling it with too much brown lard.

The Indian rose ponderously, shook hands with Steven, and said, "Your good friend Tiger come see Pierton. You tell him come." He smiled broadly and sat down again.

Steven had seen no dugout on the shore; the Indian must have landed on the far side of the island. The Seminoles had a way of getting up and down this part of the state, an inland way through the Everglades. Driven back there in the war made upon them, they never spoke of their secret route and would let no white man know. Steven asked, "How long you been here, Tiger?"

"One day."

"Why didn't you come in to the lake?"

"No good. No get wy-oh-mey at lake." Tiger heaved with silent laughter. It jiggled the gold-plated watch chain, to which there was no watch attached, that ran across the white-man's waistcoat he wore. Numerous safety pins, fastened to this as decorations, glittered and shone.

Steven supposed he could trust the Indian, even though he didn't know him from long standing. Seminoles were too simple to be very tricky. And Tiger, with reason to be in his debt, had previously shown his good will by bringing him and Doc a whole young buck.

Steven asked Tiger if he knew the beachcombers and Tiger replied, "Know him." Steven inquired if he knew where they lived in the Glades, and Tiger said again, "Know him."

But when he asked Tiger to tell him where it was, and requested him to lead men to it, the Indian shook his head. "Long time ago one time," he explained, "I show him where to put house. I show him way to get, way to go out. I tell him nobody know from me."

This put a new light on Tiger, seeming to align him with the combers. "They're bad men, Tiger," Steven told him.

"Him bad," Tiger agreed. "Me good, ojus."

In this way did the Indian indicate that he would not break his promise. Though a disappointment to Steven, it was a recommendation for Tiger.

The Indian spoke again. Indiscriminately, he referred to one or more of the beachcombers in the singular. Steven knew he meant Theron when he revealed, "You make arm sick in fight. No good now, like this." Tiger illustrated by hanging his left arm over the side of the barrel chair and letting it flop uselessly. The silent laughter shook him again.

He had really hurt Theron, then. Without medical attention the arm probably hadn't set properly. That meant he had made an active enemy. Steven had watched for the combers to appear again. This told him why they hadn't. Theron was waiting for his arm to heal. Now Steven was sure he would strike, the more viciously because of the injury.

Tiger corroborated this. "Him no good for you. You look with eyes, all time. You keep boats so no see."

Fourteen

STEVEN RAGED BECAUSE his sandy highway along the sea was no longer a place of complete freedom. When he had passengers now he didn't dare sleep them out on the open beach the second night. Instead, he took them into the scrub, hiding out, to be eaten and bitten by the hordes of sandflies and mosquitoes. With the coming of the summer rains, these were nearly intolerable, and Steven had to accept without rebuttal the well-taken complaints of those who walked with him.

He was glad when the second house of refuge was completed at Fort Lauderdale. Twenty-five miles below that of the Pagets, it made two overnight stops with the spacious shelter provided by the lofts.

At the inlets he hid the skiffs more thoroughly than before, taking them farther up each river to conceal them from all sight in the dense undergrowth. Yet each time he searched them out his heart was in his throat before finding that they lay unmolested. He didn't care to swim the streams during the weeks it would take to replace a stolen boat, and some of his passengers would never have braved the varmint-infested water once.

He remained on guard as he walked, though he didn't consider likely an attack the way it had been made before. The combers, stung once in this fashion, wouldn't attempt it again. It would be by some other means, sly and mean, that they would attempt to get back at him.

They gave no sign of what this might be. He never saw them. They didn't appear on the beach during his passing. Waiting for them to act was at first tantalizing. Then it became a wish, and finally a maddening desire that baffled him and made him feel helpless.

As the summer advanced, both the sun and the rains bore down on the beach. Steven walked a shimmering ribbon of heat waves, so strong that they often created a mirage on the sand, blending the illusion of water with the real sea. The rains intensified from quick downpours in the middle of every afternoon, frequently out of a clear sky, to more extended onslaughts. Sometimes the savage little storms arrived from the land, at other times he could see them far out over the ocean heading for the shore.

Then the rain came down in blinding curtains, afterward leaving the air sticky and humid. For his passengers, Steven sought what covering he could. When alone, he kept on walking, welcoming the rain and glorying in it as it soaked him cool. The sun dried him all too quickly and he longed for another downpour, hurrying toward it when he could see one ahead.

The monotony of the beach-walking was broken in July by a play held in the Bunnell warehouse. The first Steven knew the date set for this was the evening he would be in Miami was when Adie told him. She had persuaded the people to hold it then. "I asked you if you knew how to dance," she reminded. "Now I'm going to find out."

Reference to their trip together always encouraged Steven. That was something to talk about. It was theirs, alone and apart from Sylvanus. That she had thought about him especially for the play made Steven look forward to it eagerly. He could dance, and he liked to dance.

That Wednesday afternoon he hurried as he approached the ocean beach at Miami. From far away he could see a boat sitting well up on the sand. As he neared he recognized it to be the Margaret D. Cap Jim had beached her at high tide so that she would float again on the incoming water. Her masts stood bare and her center board was drawn up. The hatch was open. With the help of the construction crew, whose tents were pitched near by, Cap Jim and Gerald were unloading the sharpie of her cargo.

Cap Jim hailed Steven. "Give us a hand!" he called. "I want to catch that tide as soon as it's in to get up to Jax for another load."

Steven joined in the work. He kept looking at the sky in which the moon was already taking a sharp outline. He didn't want to be late for the dancing. He didn't want Sylvanus to get ahead of him.

He worked fast, hurrying men with whom he received timbers as they passed steadily over the rail of the sharpie. He sweated as he carried and ran back each time for the next load.

"I'm in a hurry," Cap Jim told him, "but not that much. Way you're acting you'd think you couldn't wait to get to that girl of yours over to Miami."

Gerald cackled. It was the first sound out of him in connection with Steven. Because Steven hadn't made his flower work with Adie, the little Conch held him in contempt and refused to speak to him.

It was well past eight that evening before the unloading was completed. Water lapped up the flat stern of the Margaret D. There was time for a hurried meal, but Steven didn't wait for it. As he prepared to cross the reef by the light of the moon, Cap Jim asked, "Ain't you going to have any supper?"

"They're having fiddlers tonight," Steven explained, "and I got an hour's row ahead of me to get there."

"I was right about the girl!" Cap Jim roared. Then he demanded, "Why didn't you say so before?"

The two fiddles were going together, warm and high, when Steven arrived at the trading post. He dumped the mail unceremoniously behind the counter. With the play under way, Bunnell would refuse to distribute it until the next day.

Cleaned up, his hair brushed, his shoes on his feet, Steven made his way to the warehouse door. Only then did he notice how thick were the mosquitoes. They filled the air, buzzing softly, drawn to the heat exuding through the screen door. Outside, braving the insects in the interests of a bottle, stood a group of men. The sheriff greeted Steven, "Here's the man who set the date."

Another man guffawed, "He ain't set the date for something else."

"I'm holding off," Steven replied, "till you wear yourself to a shadow worrying about it."

The sheriff was stationed at the door to operate it to keep out the mosquitoes. Steven reflected that this was about all Oat McCarty was good for. The sheriff grasped the knob of the door, warning, "Ready!"

Steven knew the formula.

"Jump!" The door was jerked open.

Steven leaped inside as the door was slammed shut against the insects.

Goods and merchandise had been piled high on all sides of the warehouse, making a dance floor down its length lighted by two kerosene lamps hung from the ceiling. Sperm oil had been rubbed on the boards to make them smooth, but even so dust rose in the suffocating air as a set of eight couples, with Dan Bunnell calling, went through its gyrations.

People had come from up and down the bay, and the few who lived inland were here. Dressed in their best, they looked like Sunday. There was room for only part of them to dance at one time. Most of them stood, others sat on packing cases. The only two chairs were for the fiddlers.

One of these was a gangling man, a sponger who also kept turtle crawls on the bay shore. He had a regulation violin which he held solemnly under his chin. He sawed at it in lively fashion. The other musician was the boat-builder from the Grove, a slim, wise-looking little man with a white goatee. The Professor had his own invention made from a tremendous coconut. The neck of his instrument was of wood, it had two strings, and he used a violin bow to make sounds fully as sweet and piercing as the manufactured fiddle working at his side.

> "*Dip for the oyster, dive for the clam,*
> *Now take a dip for the promised land.*"

Steven, craning his neck to see Adie, found her at once. She was being swung by Sylvanus. She was his partner. As she came around, Steven caught her glance. Her face, already lighted, became brighter, and she waved a hand at him before being whirled about. Steven liked the way she moved, the way her dress swirled out, the way her feet barely touched the floor before she was on and gone.

Bunnell brought the figure to a close:

> *"Promenade all around the hall;*
> *You know where and I don't care;*
> *Throw her in the old armchair."*

The dancers, breathless, stopped to make way for others. Another set formed under the trader's direction.

Adie stood with her back to Steven while she spoke with Sylvanus. Steven had a confidence on a dance floor. Women on it had always seemed impersonal, contact with them solely for the enjoyment of executing the figures. He went up to Adie, took her hand, and pulled her into line before she knew who it was who led her. Then, laughing protest, she told him, "You haven't even asked me. And I'm too tired to—"

The music started and he marched off with her. He started to explain what had made him late, lost her before he was finished, and completed the story when she came back to him. Then he asked, "How's your ma getting on?" She was swung away without time to answer, but gave it when she came around again, "The heat isn't good for her."

It was no effort to carry her along. Her slim body responded to the slightest suggestion of movement. There was joy in the swing of her. She wore Gerald's flower in her hair and the puce-colored dress in which Steven had first seen her as a woman and always pictured her. Her face was flushed and her eyes were quick and merry. In them Steven could see that she liked him to dance with.

"Gents bow, the ladies know how;
Turn your opposite twice once;
Kick her in the shins
And knock her down."

The women took little filigree steps while staying in one spot. They put their arms about the shuffling men's shoulders to catch the hand of the next woman. Steven could feel only Adie's arm about him; that of the other woman might not have been there.

Steven saw it was a surprise to Adie when Emily Bunnell made a proposal that seemed to have been agreed upon in advance by the others. The two sisters had joined the dancing, actively and spryly, displaying an intense enthusiasm. Each had been the partner of Sylvanus, and watching them, Steven saw their set, white faces when they touched the boomer. Now Emily, her voice cracking with excitement, cried, "Dance the men down! Them two!" She pointed first to Steven and then to Sylvanus.

Others took up the cry. "Dance them down! Dance them off their feet!"

The rest of the men on the floor retired to the side of the warehouse as the fiddles struck up with new life.

Sylvanus called, "I don't know what you mean."

Steven grinned and told him, "You'll soon enough find out."

"I don't know what to do." Sylvanus spoke to the crowd rather than to Steven.

"You'll get it done for you," Steven informed him.

The women appointed themselves the partners of the two men for a round dance. Each danced with one of them for a furious minute and then dropped out, to have another and ready woman take her place instantly. In this way, taking turns, they rested while the men being danced down were kept at it continually. It would keep up until one of them stopped dead in his tracks and could move no more.

At first Adie didn't want to be one of those wearing down

her two suitors. Too much attention was being drawn to her as it was. But when she was pushed into the circle she took it in good part, grabbing Sylvanus and turning him as vigorously as the others.

Bunnell shouted, and everyone knew what he meant, "Winner sees her home!"

Steven, over Clara Bunnell's bony shoulder, called to Sylvanus, "That's me."

Past the cinnamon of Adie's hair, Sylvanus corrected, "It's I."

A man from the sidelines advised him, "Good grammer ain't going to put starch in your legs!"

Steven watched Sylvanus moving confidently, gracefully, almost without effort. A quarter of an hour after the contest began he showed no signs of fatigue.

Steven himself was dubious about winning against him. He had been tired when he arrived. But he grinned at each fresh woman who came to him, and kept up with her. He put extra spring in his steps when it came Adie's turn with him.

The sheriff and the other men came in to watch the fun. Bets were made. Sylvanus was favored because most people believed Steven wouldn't last after his three days of walking. If they had known of his work on the beach, and his going without supper, Steven was sure no one at all would back him.

He began to weaken before Sylvanus showed any signs of it. But the women would let neither of them slow; they carried them along, increasing the pace instead of slackening it. Wobbling on his feet, it seemed to Steven that the Bunnell sisters attacked like animals eager to make a kill. Emily called for the music to go faster.

The fiddlers, instead of obeying, faltered, and then took turns, one resting while the other played. The Professor's coconut violin began to scratch and hit sour notes, which caused someone to remark, "Looks like the fiddlers is going to be danced down instead of the men."

Steven determined to last out. After winning, he would take

Adie home and then ask her to marry him. His resolve gave him all the strength he had left. His whole body cried out to stop, to rest. Then a look at Adie or at the now staggering Sylvanus made him keep on. He didn't know how long he had been going through motions of which he was hardly conscious. Someone called out that it was half an hour. It seemed a day later when three-quarters was announced.

Finally the women began to tire. At that, to end it, Clara Bunnell cried, "Whirl them! Whirl them about!"

Steven found himself being turned, rapidly, around and around. He was dizzy after the first few turns. The sound of the music went away after several minutes of it and then there were only strange noises and a blur of shouting, grimacing faces.

He was almost ready to give up Adie in exchange for the blessed relief of stopping when he caught a glimpse of Sylvanus. Sylvanus took the whirling without seeming to mind it. Steven decided that he could do the same. He made his feet move against the mounting dizziness, hanging on to the women, unable to recognize them.

He didn't know how or when the end came. He knew only that he was at last left alone and that he was lurching about trying to keep his balance. The fiddles had stopped and people were laughing and crying out and clapping and Sylvanus, strangely, was sitting on the floor, gasping, his body held at an odd angle, and laughing himself.

Steven was slapped on the back. Someone shouted, "Winner takes a kiss, too!" The cry came from other voices. "Winner takes a kiss!"

Still dizzy, Steven found himself before Adie. She looked at him uncertainly. She turned, and tried to make her way out, but the crowd closed in, barring her way. Then she stood, a flush in her cheeks.

"You're the winner, Stevie! Take it!"

Steven realized fully what was required of him. He went cold with dread and fright. He wanted to kiss Adie, but not here, before everybody. He could barely look at her standing there, unwilling yet inviting.

"Take it! Take it!"

Then Steven saw the tiny smile on Adie's lips. It seemed to challenge his courage. He forced himself to start toward her.

He was too late. It was Sylvanus who moved in ahead of him and took advantage of the crowd's advice. On his feet again, the loser stepped quickly to Adie. Before she or anyone else knew what was happening, he had taken her in his arms. The kiss he implanted full on her lips lasted as long as it took Adie, in her surprise, to realize and twist from him.

Now she stood shocked and outraged, while the crowd roared.

It wasn't the look on Adie's face that made Steven jump forward. It was the sight of Adie in Sylvanus's arms and the picture of his mouth on hers.

He grasped Sylvanus by the lapel of his coat, swinging him around. In his anger, Steven gave him no chance. He hit him straight in the face.

Sylvanus went down.

He stayed for a moment, while he recovered and glared up at Steven. When he scrambled to his feet, women cried out shrilly. Sylvanus made a lunge at Steven, who was ready for him. But the other men interfered, holding Sylvanus, grasping Steven, getting between the warriors, breaking up the fight.

Steven relaxed. Hands loosened their hold on him. He looked about. Adie was no longer there.

As he shouldered his way out, a woman observed, "Shame!" Steven was surprised to know that the sympathy was with Sylvanus. People were angry at him for spoiling the fun.

Outside, Adie was not in sight. He could see no one in the strong moonlight. Only the mosquitoes were to be felt.

Stepping away from the warehouse, he listened. He was sure he could hear the sound of footsteps from the path leading to the Titus homestead.

He strode after her. She was a dim figure ahead of him, then,

at his side, a plain one. They walked in silence for a full minute. Each worked at mosquitoes. She seemed to take out on
them more than a full measure of annoyance. Steven knew this
was for him. The little resolve remaining to ask for her drained
away and left him empty. He murmured, "I better see you
home."

Staring straight ahead, she told him, "You don't need to take
that part of it."

He kept on walking with her. Once, when she stumbled over
a root, he caught her arm to steady her. She jerked away.

He wondered if her anger could come from his not having
taken the kiss when he should have, for putting her in the position where Sylvanus stole it and making the people laugh. He
could fathom the last part of that, but not the first.

He learned that wasn't all of it when she spoke again. "Fighting," she accused. "I've never had men fight over me."

Steven felt properly guilty.

"Before everybody," she added.

He felt humbled and wrong.

"And you hit him like—like any rough."

Steven bridled at her standing up for Sylvanus. "He didn't
have any call to do that."

"You didn't have any right to fight."

He felt chastened again. "Yes, ma'm," he said.

At his address he saw her face turn to him quickly, and
then away. She said nothing more until they reached her house.
Then she mounted the steps and stood there above him and lectured him again.

She didn't sound as angry as before. She might have disposed
of the first things she felt and the things expected of her, and
now was speaking more thoughtfully. She might even have
been faintly amused, a little flattered and delighted. But her
words were the same, and Steven couldn't tell for sure. She
stopped and seemed to wait for him to say something.

"Yes, ma'm," he said again.

She stared at him. She slapped a mosquito. She cried with

exasperation, "Oh, Steven!" She turned and went into the house, closing the door after her.

Steven couldn't figure it all out as he walked back to the trading post. He had heard men say women were queer. He suspected they must be. He liked the look on Adie's face when she was mad; it was so earnest, animated, and determined that it was a little bit absurd.

He knew that and one other thing. He wanted her more than ever.

Fifteen

IN AUGUST, DEWEY DURGAN, his face purple and his hand shaking, signed the Deacon's temperance petition. The Deacon's efforts had already made the lake community dry, driving Durgan to Pratt's Geneva Gin, and now the entire county was threatened. After putting his name to the document, Durgan shocked ladies gathered in the store by announcing, "I'm voting against it in November, and I hope all right-thinking people will follow suit."

Another petition was circulating up and down the northern end of the county. This was instigated by Doc, with the support of nearly every settler. It asked for a vote on the location of the county seat. Too long, it was felt, had the upstart Miami had the best of it with the heart of politics located there. It was time it came to the other end, where it rightfully belonged.

Doc's own motivation was not entirely one of community spirit. As a county commissioner, he was forced to travel to Miami several times each year. Besides detesting the trip, he had to close the store while he was gone, for he wouldn't trust his brother to keep it open. Doc wanted the meeting place closer to home.

Now there was scheduled a meeting of the commissioners and Doc was to take the two petitions to Miami. Cap Jim paid no attention to the order to transport him, as he usually did. Cap had one more trip to make for the government, and he would be on his way upcountry at the time of the meeting. Storming about this, Doc made arrangements to be picked up by a schooner bringing the two commissioners from the north end of the county.

Packed and ready on the morning the boat was to arrive, Doc fumed at the heavy sea running. What the schooner coming down would do about getting over the bar at the inlet was questionable.

Quimby, who watched on the beach, came to the store to report, "He went on past."

Doc had a tantrum about skippers not having more respect for county commissioners. "He might have waited out there at least one day for it to calm. Now I've got to walk that beach with Stevie."

Steven, when he returned in the afternoon, told Doc he would walk him only at night. "The daytime heat would kill you. It near about kills me. You can't even touch the dry sand with your feet." Steven was a living example of what the sun was like on the open beach during the summer. His skin had taken on the rich hue of a seabean, so deep a color that he looked like an Indian.

To arrive at the meeting on Tuesday, they would have to start that same night, with Steven taking no sleep. And Doc had to revise his luggage, traveling with nothing except the clothes on his back and discarding the package of medicines he had wrapped to take along.

This last he refused to do. "Them people down there will come around clamoring for what I haven't got as it is," he said, "with most of them needing only a good purge. And you yourself want me to have the tonic you asked me about for the mother of that girl of yours."

"I'll take that in my sack," Steven told him. "But I won't carry the rest when it gets too heavy for you."

Just before they closed and locked the store, they soaped themselves as a preventive against the attack of sandflies that would be on the beach. They covered their faces, necks, hands, and legs with a thick lather which they let dry. It was stiff and hard on their skins.

At the beach not a breath of air stirred. There was light, a faint glowing that seemed to come from nowhere, but was enough for them to see their way dimly. Occasionally the water swirled with phosphorus as something swift darted in it. Compared with the day, the night was almost chilly as they walked along.

Yet it wasn't cool enough to discourage the insects. At times they were so thick that they breathed them. The soap mostly kept them from other parts, but the nipping midges got into their nostrils, their ears, even into their eyes. Only by walking briskly were they able to keep them from finding the cracks made in their soap coverings as they moved.

When they stopped to rest, they made a smudge fire by piling green beach grass over the flames. When the smoke became worse than the sandflies, they went on. Doc trudged behind Steven, puffing and grunting complaint. Steven could hear him shifting the medicine package from shoulder to shoulder; the bottles tinkled like high-toned bells in the night.

Finally Doc stopped and announced, "I can't go another step, Stevie."

Steven, who had gone on a little ahead, went back to him. "Unless you decided this is where you want to be buried," he said, "you'll go a lot more steps." Saying nothing more, he took the medicine package from him and, carrying it, went on.

Doc followed, muttering, "I don't know what brought me to this pioneer country. If I had it to do over, I'd never come near the place."

He was able to grunt only weak greetings at the Pagets when Steven dragged him into the station in the morning. After washing the caked soap off their skins, both of them lay like logs in the loft until late afternoon, when they descended to partake of supper. At the table Doc peered at Della over his spectacles.

She sat, proud rather than ashamed of her appearance. This was, to say the least, extraordinary, for the second life within her bloomed frankly. She was to have her baby in November. Steven, through the weeks of watching her body become miraculously misshapen, took it as not a thing to dwell upon with thought or sight. He tried to ignore and take no notice of it, and the more he did so the more conscious he became of it.

Doc gave his judgment to Jesse. "She's still mighty nice-looking—outside of what you done to her."

Laughing, Della turned to her husband for him to defend her. Jesse said, "She's the best-looking she's ever been, right now."

"What you going to do when it comes?" Doc asked Della.

Linda gave the answer. Pointing her fork at Jesse, she said, "I had him without help. I speck she kin do the same. Iffen she can't, I kin bring up enough aid to show her how."

"I don't need any help from you," Della retorted.

"You mought," Linda warned, "afore you're through."

"I 'mought!'" Della mocked. "Well, I mought not."

"Girl," Linda shrilled, "you talk like you know everything, an' nobody kin—"

"I told you to keep shut," Jesse informed his mother, "till it comes. Then you can make all the fuss you want."

Linda opened her mouth to go on, but Jesse said sternly, "Now I mean what I say."

They didn't have to soap themselves that night because the southeast trade wind had sprung up briskly enough to drive the sandflies to cover. Between the two inlets Steven came upon signs that a turtle had laid its eggs. He dug at a mound showing it had been built and patted down with flippers. It turned out to be a mock nest, made to fool bears and other animals. Above it, to one side, Steven found the real nest, and uncovered a cache of several hundred round white eggs. Before spreading sand over them again he took out twenty and asked Doc:

"You hungry·enough for a taste of these to risk building a fire and letting the combers know we're along here?"

"Let them come out," Doc challenged. He yelled the words at the dark wall of the scrub above the beach.

"Don't invite them so loud," Steven ordered. "They might take you up, and then where'd you be?"

Steven made a batter of the eggs by beating their contents with his knife in the coffee-boil. Then he cooked slapjacks. They were so light as to be feathery, and in the cool of the night they devoured the delicacy while peering beyond their fire at the scrub.

Theron and his men made no appearance. Steven had heard that the combers a week ago stole into Miami for supplies, and were unmolested. When he charged the sheriff with this, Oat said he didn't know anything about it. Dan Bunnell admitted that maybe the men had been there. "There ain't anything to prove on them," the trader said, "so we couldn't do anything about it." Not, Steven thought, when Bunnell was selling goods to the combers.

The morning they reached Miami the schooner bearing the other two commissioners from the north end of the county was anchored off the mouth of the river. They, with the skipper, hung over the rail to greet Steven and Doc as they rowed past. Doc, disheveled, footsore, and aching in every bone, waved weakly to them and had no strength to berate the skipper.

In the trading post, Doc summoned enough energy to storm to Bunnell, "I wish the Spanish or the English or the French had kept Florida when they had it. I ain't coming here to a meeting again."

"You like it every chance you get," the trader taunted. "So

you can hold one of your medicine shows in my store. And make a profit on your snake oils. I ought to charge you."

Doc looked with scorn at the few bottles to be seen on Bunnell's shelves. "If you knew enough about it to put in a real pharmacy yourself," he retorted, "everybody around here wouldn't look as if they're dying."

With Doc, Steven slept until afternoon. Then, when the people began to come in for their mail, getting to know it had arrived a whole day earlier than usual, he went out with Doc to the store. He awaited Adie there while Doc held court with his bottles.

People swarmed about him with their ills. Some of them had ordered cures and were expecting them. While the others waited and listened with interest, Doc lectured each one. He let out no secrets, for in so small a place everyone knew the troubles of everyone else.

The Bunnell sisters came into the store. Instead of patent medicine, they were concerned with Steven. They made directly for him, startling him when they appeared before him like a committee come with an important message. Clara delivered it at once. Triumphantly, she said, "He's asked her to marry him."

It was a moment before Steven understood what she meant. Then a stab of fear went through him. He had never been able to believe that Sylvanus would ask for marriage. He hadn't counted on it.

At the look on his face, Emily demanded gleefully, "What do you think of that?"

He wanted to ask them what Adie had answered. But he couldn't have put the question if they had stayed to be asked. They marched out again abruptly.

Sylvanus wasn't about. That, Steven decided, was a bad sign. The thought that Adie had accepted him was not real to him. It simply couldn't be.

Just then Adie came in.

He read at once in her face and manner that she had not

accepted Sylvanus. Or at least he fancied that he could. Since the night of the play she had been the least bit cool to him, as if not quite satisfied with him or being a bit disappointed in him. Now she was as happy as before at seeing him. Her eyes opened wide to show the twinkle in their gray depths, her smile and greeting were warm.

Even so Steven began to doubt. She might be simply surprised at seeing him earlier in the week than usual. She might be treating him gently, so as to ease the news to come.

Hurriedly he gave her the bottle of medicine for her mother, saying, "Here's the Harter's Iron Tonic. And your mail."

She took them both, glancing briefly at the letters, gratefully at the bottle, and then as appreciatively at him. Her eyes went from him to Doc who came from across the room to say, "Here's the boy who turned into a girl." He peered at her more closely above his spectacles. He showed how impressed he was when he said unbelievingly, "You ain't the same person. It can't be."

Small white teeth flashed between Adie's lips. "Steven can tell you."

"I still say," Doc went on, "he's been fooling me." He examined her again. "But I'll say, too, he picked himself something good."

Steven squirmed. Adie's lashes closed over her eyes once and then came up again. She didn't look at Steven, but at Doc. She held up Harter's Iron Tonic, telling him, "I know it will help my mother."

"Cures want of appetite, indigestion, lack of strength, and tired feeling," Doc told her. "Bones, muscles, and nerves receive new force. Enlivens the mind and supplies brain power."

Adie became sober. "It's the weather that troubles her now. When will the heat and the rains be over?"

Before Doc could answer, someone called him loudly. He left without replying and it was Steven who told her, "You got to wait till after hurricane time, which is now through September. When the first northeaster blows you'll know it's over, sometime along in October. Next year your ma will be all right—it takes a summer season for some folks to get used to the climate."

He was anxious to get her out of the trading post. She responded to his moving toward the door, going with him. They walked out of earshot of the store before he said, "I won't be seeing you tonight, because Doc wants me to go to the meeting."

He knew what he had to do. Now, today, immediately, he must ask her to marry him. He had never expected to be faced with the necessity this way. He had waited another opportunity, such as the play had offered but not finally brought. It didn't seem right now. It wasn't as he pictured and planned it. Hurried, forced, and wrong, he wasn't even sure he could do it.

The thought that it might be too late already made him panicky. Always she stilled his tongue and was a crisis taking away all coolheadedness. She prevented him from thinking straight. Even though the sun was slanting away its fierce heat, he wiped his face with the upper part of his sleeve where it was rolled. He blurted, "He's asked for you?"

He watched her out of the corner of his eye as they walked along. Looking straight in front of her, Adie nodded.

That was all he could say right away. They entered between the trees leading to her people's homestead, where the clearing in the town ended and the way became thick with undergrowth.

"Adie, I . . ." He began again. "All along I—if you want to think about—before you . . ." He stopped, floundering, and then ended with an unintentional rush, "You ain't going to take him?"

Adie stopped and they faced each other. The twitch at the corners of her mouth did not last for long. When it stopped it was as if she had decided not to laugh at him. He thought that a slight mist came to her eyes. Certainly she was serious and tender when she said, "I can think only of my mother until she's well, Steven. She needs me."

She spoke simply, and that was all she had to say. There was only the slightest hesitation before she turned and continued along the path.

Steven didn't follow. He remained rooted with sudden relief. She wasn't going to take Sylvanus.

At least she hadn't taken him yet.

Or wasn't ready to admit it.

Which was it?

A realization, worse than all the others, struck him. Still he hadn't asked her for himself. And with each try and failure it became more difficult for the next time.

Sixteen

THE FIVE COUNTY COMMISSIONERS were gathered in the trading post. Besides Doc and Bunnell, there were sandy-haired Henry Pinder from Elliott's Key, a small community some miles down Biscayne Bay; red-bearded William Baker from Waveland at the north tip of the county; and tall, angular Ernest Maple from Jupiter.

In addition to these was Timothy Piggott, the county clerk. Piggott was a nervous little man with a pinched face who continually looked to Bunnell as if for advice about drawing every breath. He was among those known to have gone in with Sylvanus by turning his land into tourist lots. There was some question about how he acquired the land in the first place, but keeping the records as he did, it was felt that not much could be done about it.

Sylvanus had not put in an appearance all evening. It bothered Steven, and made him feel that he could be putting in his own time better elsewhere instead of learning something about county politics.

Bunnell kept looking at his watch long after it was time to set out for the courthouse. He appeared to be worried. As chairman, it was up to him to get the party under way. But he spoke no word about this. Piggott fussed with two unlighted lanterns, glancing from them to the trader.

"We're all here," Doc pointed out.

"Come on," Baker said through his beard, "what we waiting on?"

"Directly," Bunnell muttered, "directly."

The other commissioners regarded him curiously, but said nothing more for the moment. The trader kept his eyes on the door and looked at his watch again. Five minutes passed.

"If this meeting ain't going to start," Pinder announced, "I'm going home again."

Reluctantly, Bunnell told Piggott, "I suppose you can light the lanterns."

Piggott, looking like a scared rabbit, put a match to the wicks. When they were burning steadily, he picked up one and gave the other to Bunnell.

Led slowly by the trader, the party moved out of the store and to the river's edge. Here they were greeted by Abaco when they boarded the ferry. Even Abaco seemed to be a part of the conspiracy of delay in starting the meeting, for after Bunnell spoke a few whispered words to him, he took his time about going to the passengers for their fares.

Doc demanded of Bunnell, "You mean to say you're charging the commissioners to get across?"

The trader, after a glance at Steven who stood by the wooden rail of the barge, replied, "If it was me alone, of course I wouldn't do it. But it's a Company thing."

Doc snorted. "You don't need to look at Stevie. Anybody with sense knows who's this Company of yours. You and that Hurley fellow. The people of Miami are going to wake up some day and—" Doc grabbed the rail as Abaco started pulling on the ferry rope, getting the vessel under way with a jerk.

When they landed on the other side of the river and all had stepped to the bank, Abaco was sent back immediately, again after whispered instructions from Bunnell.

By the light of the lanterns, and fighting mosquitoes drawn to them, they made their way through the grove of palms standing on the north side of the river. Just beyond stood the long, low, single-storied building that served as the Dade County Courthouse.

Old Fort Dallas was the only structure of age in Miami. Here and there the outer plaster had fallen away, sometimes from the splatter of a bullet. The pock-marked gray stone that showed beneath was grimy with smoke and weathering. The thick timbers of the door at which Piggott fumbled with a huge iron key were cracked and worm-eaten, as were the shutters on the narrow windows.

They entered a square, low-ceilinged room. It was bare except for a table standing along its center, a half dozen chairs at this, a few scattered benches, and an ancient cabinet which reached nearly the height of the room. The air was damp and musty, and the mosquitoes, following the light in, seemed to favor it. The commissioners slapped and cursed as the lanterns were placed on the table and they seated themselves.

Bunnell took a chair at its head. Still moving as leisurely as before, Piggott unlocked the cabinet, and began to take out the ledger books and papers comprising the county records, which he piled on the table.

Steven seated himself on a bench at the side of the room. By now he had figured out the unwillingness to start the meeting on the parts of the trader and the county clerk. He sat watching to see how far they would go with it.

The records were ready. The commissioners waited. Bunnell, instead of calling the meeting to order, again looked at his watch. He coughed, slapped a mosquito, and said with forced joviality, "It appears to me this is a meeting of all the bugs in the county instead of the commissioners."

Pinder, while Doc fumed at the delay, accepted the bait. "This ain't nothing. Why, down in the Keys folks has got to put overalls on their mules to keep them from being killed by the skeeters."

Baker, wagging his beard with appreciation, recounted, "I been driving sometimes and the mosquitoes would light so thick on my horse you couldn't have told me what color it was. I been at farmhouses to dinner where there'd be so much of a smudge to drive the critters out that I couldn't see the persons sitting across from me."

Steven couldn't resist offering a tale of his own. "In a crocodile hole I seen a big old croc open his mouth and keep his jaws apart until the inside was black with them. Then he snaps his jaws together and runs his tongue around inside and swallows. He keeps that up until he gets a good full meal."

Maple spoke up for the first time. "Don't be afraid to tell the whole truth while you are about it, gentlemen. Now I've had my chamber windows so covered with mosquitoes that not a ray of light could get in, and as a result I've slept through most of a day, thinking all the time it was night."

The chuckles that greeted this died away as the sound of footsteps was heard outside. The commissioners, wondering, looked toward the door.

It was Sylvanus Hurley. Jauntily, he greeted them, glancing with satisfaction at Bunnell and Piggott. "I see you haven't started yet. If I may be permitted to sit and listen?" Without waiting for a reply he seated himself on one of the benches.

Bunnell rapped on the table with his knuckles. "The meeting will come to order."

"So it was him you waited for," Doc stated.

The other commissioners stared thoughtfully, but Bunnell paid no attention. He ordered Piggott to read the minutes of the last meeting.

Before Piggott could begin, Doc interrupted. Pointing a finger at Sylvanus he said, "He ain't got any right to be here."

The commissioners sat up in their chairs a little, their interest activated by the question Doc raised.

"You're out of order, Mister Bethune," Bunnell informed him.

"I still say he ain't got any right to be here," Doc insisted.

"We ain't ever made any ruling about the meetings being open or private," Bunnell argued.

From his bench Sylvanus offered, "I don't wish to cause difficulty, gentlemen. I'll willingly retire."

"You got as much right to be here as Pierton," Bunnell decreed. He addressed the commissioners. "I say the public ought to be let in—"

"Let them both stay and let's get on with the meeting," suggested Pinder.

Doc partially subsided. "Holding up the meeting till he got here," he muttered. "He ain't to speak."

"*They* ain't to speak," said Bunnell.

The formal meeting began. Steven, delegated to silence, listened with one half of his mind and with the other half wondered if the business that had made Sylvanus late had been with Adie. Piggott's voice stopped, that of Bunnell and others began, and Piggott started to scratch with a pen. The lamps fluttered as unsuspecting insects flew close over them, were singed to a crisp and their bodies fell into the flames.

Arrangements were discussed, voted on, and adopted for the general election that would put new men in the county offices. It was then that Doc brought forth his two petitions. Steven noted that the concentration of Sylvanus on the proceedings quickened when Doc passed the papers to Bunnell.

The trader read in a resentful tone from the first of them. "'A petition for an election to decide whether the sale of intoxicating liquors, wines or beer shall be prohibited in Dade County.' " Bunnell flipped over the pages and said, "It's signed by fifty-three registered voters, the said number being the legal one-third or over of the registered voters in said county. I suppose we got to accept it whether or not we want to."

Maple's voice was the only one enthusiastic as temperance was entered as one of the election issues.

Bunnell took up the second of the petitions as if it were something hot that would burn his fingers. His voice showed how much he was trying to hold his temper as this time he read:

" 'Petition for an election to locate the county site in and for Dade County during the next ten years."

The trader looked up. His plump body seemed to explode all over when he said, "Everybody knows what that means! You lake people think you can get the county site away from us. Well, you won't do it! We always had more population than you and we got still more now with—"

"That'll be decided at the election," Doc interrupted.

Watching Sylvanus, Steven thought he looked regretful at the trader's outburst. Bunnell, containing himself with effort, went on, "Signed by fifty-six registered voters, which is over one-third of them in the county." Contemptuously, he admitted, "It's the same with this as the other."

"Except," Baker pointed out, "we want this one."

"*You* want it," Bunnell retorted, "and Bethune and Maple want it. But we'll outvote you all down the line."

"The chairman," Doc reproved, "is supposed to hold the meeting, not a political argument. We got two months to do all of that we want."

The argument started immediately after the meeting was adjourned. While Piggott scuttled to put away the records in the cabinet, Bunnell cornered Baker and Maple, with Pinder joining them. Sylvanus attached himself to Doc and Steven, with Steven having little to say to him. He was engendering an active dislike for the man, and felt no longer civil to him.

Sylvanus, on the other hand, always seemed to take an enjoyment out of being Steven's rival, and he continued to find pleasure in it. The blow Steven had struck him appeared to make little difference. There was, behind his eyes, only more of a mocking.

"So you made a nuisance of yourself on the beach," Doc told Sylvanus, "and you're making a bigger nuisance of yourself here."

Sylvanus laughed, to indicate how good-naturedly ridiculous was Doc's remark. "You'll really find out in the election," he said. "You don't realize everything we're doing here."

"I got a good idea," Doc replied.

Sylvanus ignored the implications in this remark. "Why, the Company has brought seventeen new landowners. That's besides the people who came in the regular way and who bought land. And," he added significantly, "are voters. Do you think you can compete with that? Of course you can't."

"We'll give you a run for it," Doc said grimly.

"More and more," Sylvanus continued, "people are realizing the advantages here. And more and more are the old settlers seeing how much better it is to turn their land to lots." It was for Steven's benefit that he made his next announcement. "I've just come from convincing Mr. Titus. For some time he has seen the light, but up until now he has not thoroughly understood the arrangement the Company makes to handle land. That is, how profitable it can be. When a careful man like that comes in with us—"

"Look out," warned Doc, "you don't take in more than you can swallow and get choked."

"We're taking everything we can get hold of," said Sylvanus, "and not stopping just around here. That reminds me. Perhaps you or Steven can tell me something of a parcel up in your end of the county." He looked at them slowly before he named it. "It's an island—called Hypoluxo."

Steven's heart went still. He could feel the blood mounting to his face and the rage surging inside him. Doc looked startled, and then furious. Shaking his finger at Sylvanus, he began to shout, "Don't you touch that! Don't you think you can—"

Holding himself to quiet, Steven cut in, asking Sylvanus, "What about it?"

Doc's cry had stopped the discussion at the other side of the room. The commissioners, and Piggott, attended Sylvanus's reply.

"Why," he explained easily, "our investigations showed it to be an attractive piece. There will be people coming to the coast who will want entire islands for themselves. This one, if I recall correctly, was homesteaded once but the Notice of Final Proof never filed. I thought you might know—"

Still quietly, Steven said, "I know. Hypoluxo belongs to me. It was left to me."

Sylvanus's surprise was well taken. "To you? But there's no record."

"I don't care about records. You found out it was mine and now you're trying to do me out of it."

"I had no dream you had any claim to it," Sylvanus disavowed. "If I had, naturally we wouldn't be having the title searched so we can put in our application to take it over."

"You ain't going to do that now," Steven told him evenly. He could feel the others listening, and Doc waiting.

"I'm afraid it's gone too far to stop. You see, it isn't mine to say alone, but—"

"—a Company thing," Steven finished for him. The silence in the room was tight and became tighter until he went on, "And you're the big part of the Company. I'm wanting to know but one thing right now: are you ready to take up where we left off at the play?"

Sylvanus regarded him coolly. He began to remove his coat, saying, "Just as ready as you are, Steven."

It was Doc now who contained himself. Pushing between them, he told Steven, "That ain't any way to do. Nothing like that will settle it, no matter how much it would help this sharper."

The others at the same time intervened, coming forward, with Bunnell decrying having a fight at a meeting of the commissioners. Doc began pulling Steven toward the door. "Don't you do it, now. Come along. If you got something smart against you, you just got to be smarter." Baker and Maple also urged Steven away.

Carrying his rage with him, Steven suffered himself to be led out. Doc affirmed, "He can't do that any more than Miami can keep the county site."

From inside the courthouse there came Bunnell's voice. "Don't you think we can't!"

Seventeen

FOR THREE SEPTEMBER DAYS heavy low clouds, without letting the sun through, made of the sky a scudding thing. It hurried to escape from some pursuing force toward which the earth itself rushed eagerly and recklessly. In their passing, the clouds, laden to bursting point, unloosed fiercely a wet cargo on everything below. Then the steady, mounting wind for a time became gusts and powerful thrusts carrying the thick, air-filling rain in slants, sometimes sending it almost horizontally over the land.

Already some of the palms along the shore were blown down, or their tops stripped of thrashing heads, to be left high bare stumps waving feebly. Other vegetation looked whipped. Some of it turned brown with burns from the sting of the heavy salt spray being carried far inland.

Steven, on the last leg of his trip before reaching the lake, was late. He walked along the base of a ten-foot wall of sand. The beach, to high up on its plain, nearly to where the vegetation began, was eaten out by the long rollers from a sea furious with wind and restive with abnormal tide. Inestimable millions of tons of sand had been sucked away, to bare in many places the limestone foundation of the earth.

The scarp was the greatest Steven had ever seen, towering above him almost unbelievably. The soft sand, dropping from the miniature cliff, was difficult to walk on. A few feet away, where the water boiled repeatedly, ravenous for more of the beach, it was impossible to make any headway at all, for here his feet sank immediately and disappeared, leaving him in sand to his ankles.

Back down the beach the barrel well had been destroyed. When Steven came along it wasn't there any more, nor was there any trace of it. Today he had arrived to see the last of Miss Neptune. The wreck was no more than splintered timbers being flung about in the roaring surf. In the midst of them the figurehead rolled over and over, intimate parts of her coyly appearing and disappearing; once Miss Neptune stuck her head out of water and seemed to look at Steven with appeal, only to say a last goodbye as she was hurried away again.

This was only the advance warning of the hurricane whose center was located somewhere far out over the ocean. Where this was, what exact direction it was taking, could only be conjectured. It might arrive tonight, tomorrow, or the next day in all its fury. It might veer off, to remain at sea, pardoning the land and allowing it peace again.

Jesse hadn't thought the full blow would hit. His station barometer read only a fraction below twenty-nine inches. And though it was still dropping, Jesse said, "Even if it keeps on down, this fancy roof the government give us will hold."

Steven himself wasn't sure about the blow. The pelicans and other birds had left the beach, but then they had sense enough to get away from any kind of danger. In the scrub the ants crawled in busy, frantic preparation, driven by some mysterious instinct to tell them what was coming. Still, he had seen them act that way when there was no unseen force torturing the growth above them. The Indians had left Miami for higher ground inland after saying the sawgrass had bloomed, which meant a hurricane. But Steven had noted that the sawgrass bloomed in places every summer and that this sign was not a true one.

He hoped he had pulled the boats at the inlets far enough on shore so that the rising water would not find them. Both rivers had begun to overflow their banks, and were swift, aggressive streams. When they reached the sea they flung a challenge into the face of the greater water there. The outcome of their struggle still had to be decided.

The thin air, when Steven struggled with the boats, had made him catch his breath and gulp his lungs fuller to get enough to carry on the work. It was thinner now as he walked along, holding himself against the wall of wind rushing unimpeded over the ocean. He wondered how Mrs. Titus was bearing up under the rarefied atmosphere the storm brought. The tonic had acted on her miraculously, bringing her strength, but the effect of the threatened big blow laid her low again.

Opposite Hypoluxo, Steven thought of Adie instead of her mother, and of Sylvanus. The boomer had convinced her that he was doing his best to have the Company stop going ahead with its plans to acquire the island. Bunnell, Sylvanus claimed, refused to listen to him. For Adie's benefit, the two of them had even staged an argument over it, Sylvanus standing up for Steven's right to Hypoluxo, the trader steadfastly refusing to give in. Steven, listening to Sylvanus's further protestations about it, could have believed them himself if he hadn't known better.

He wasn't altogether satisfied with Doc's plans for him not to lose the island. The measures seemed mild and uncertain. Doc had said the first thing to do was to find out if it was true that Uncle Charlie had never filed Notice of Final Proof for his property. If he hadn't, this meant that formal compliance with the last regulation to obtain ownership of a homestead was lacking. In this case, it would be a fine point as to whether or not Uncle Charlie could give his property to another.

Uncle Charlie himself could not be located. People had written a number of times to addresses where he might be, but received no reply. "It don't matter," Doc said. "His verbal word is as good as a written paper. A dozen people here can testify to it. But one thing we got to do is win the election. The clerk of the District Court will investigate Hypoluxo through the county officials. And with Piggott handling the papers, and Dan Bunnell over him, and that Hurley over Bunnell, we ain't got a chance."

Doc had decided that the safest thing to do would be for him to run for county clerk. Then he could look after Steven's interests. And with the courthouse moved up to the lake he could take care of the job all right along with the store. Doc shuddered to think what it would be like if he were elected and the site not moved. But there was little chance of that. They would carry the whole ticket or none at all.

Steven contented himself with that. He didn't, calmly, see what else there was to do. Except to resolve that Sylvanus would never set foot himself on Hypoluxo. He might steal it away, but Steven would prevent the profane act of his going there.

Now he bent, stooping, to shield his face from an onslaught of wind and rain. He had been soaked all day and there was no hope of keeping anything dry except the mail in his oilcloth sack, but he could turn from the drops that slashed into his face like hard pellets. Through the rain he saw something white wash up at his feet. Almost too late, as it was being carried out again, he grabbed and caught it.

The paper nautilus was nearly a foot long. Water ran off its spirals in all directions from the center. Another stream dropped from its inside, while the whole pearly surface glistened in the stormy light. All summer Steven had searched, long after the season for them. This giant had been brought up from the bottom and carried without harm over the outer reef, to sail like the Argonaut it was, to his very feet.

It was a good omen. Sylvanus had bested him in all things since the day he had presented Adie with his shell. Now Steven had something to put that to shame.

He carried it carefully and tenderly as he made his way on. It was so light that the wind fought to take it. He held the great opening of the shell away from the wind so that it would not be torn from him, protecting it with his body.

The night, made quicker by the storm, began to close in. When he was half an hour's walk from Palm Beach, Steven made his second discovery. A small keg was washed up on the beach, a quarter buried as it lay at an angle in the sand. Approaching it, Steven at first thought it no more than a piece of old wreckage vomited forth by the blow; the shore in places was littered with windrows of this. But when he reached and examined it, he straightened at once to squint out over the whipping, angry water.

He could see no sign of a ship. There was only the foaming water, rising, whitening, endlessly heaving, breathing, and fighting itself. For a long time he stared, but there was nothing to be seen in any direction.

He looked at the label on the keg again. There was curious foreign printing on it. "Vino de Jerez," it read. "España." Stamped below other letters there was, "Por Habaña."

Then he knew what a find he had for the community. A Spanish wine ship, bound for Cuba, had foundered, and her cargo, carried by the Gulf Stream, was being washed up here. To confirm this, he looked farther up the beach. He saw two more kegs like the first, and beyond them, still another. In the water, when he looked for the ship again, there were more.

With pure exuberance he risked putting the nautilus on a ledge of sand, then picked up the first keg and heaved it to the top of the scarp. Retrieving the precious shell, he hurried on.

Between the storm and Steven's report of the wine wreck, there was little sleep in Palm Beach that night. Each of the men who came through the blow for mail was called into a hurried meeting of the settlers. It was decided that nothing could be done that night, especially as most would want to remain home in case the hurricane struck. At dawn everyone would meet at the store. Then they would set out, some going north and others south. Each would tap and taste every keg and cask found, and those discovered unspoiled by sea water were to be put above the highest the tide could reach.

Dewey Durgan, his face redder than ever with pleasure, offered himself congratulations. "This is a better thing than an orange tree growing up to know how to put on fruit. What do you think, Deacon?"

"God is being good to us," the Deacon promulgated, "even though at the expense of others." He was not averse to garnering liquor from the sea to be sold for the benefit of the community.

"You going to help tomorrow?" Durgan wanted to know.

"I will do my part. Except," the Deacon made clear, "of course I shall taste but not swallow." He cleared his throat. "I hope that others will follow my example, and that we shall not be reduced to the spectacle of public drinking."

Durgan threw up his hands in horror. "Nothing like that, Deacon," he assured him. "Certainly not. Swallow but not taste. That's all any man can ask." Before the Deacon could protest, Durgan turned to Quimby and said, "It's a good thing you smeared your lard over us. Now the railroad and the launch are working and you lost your job, you can come in the wine business."

Cap Jim was called with Gerald from the Margaret D where it was tied up snugly at the dock. Cap Jim let out a whoop of delight at the news, and then was concerned over the fate of the ship and its crew.

When he announced his intention of keeping a signal fire

going on the beach all night, Steven told him, "You're crazy. You don't know what it's like out there."

"You think we're going to get it, Steve?"

"I can't tell any more than you. But you won't keep any fire going."

"I mean to try. I'd want anybody on land to do the same for me."

Steven followed Doc to bed. Chilled, he wanted no more of the weather. His quilts were damp and musty, and it was some time before the heat of his body warmed them sufficiently for him to feel comfortable. Above him was the brisk and threatening rustle of the palmetto thatch. Even though the storm didn't strike full force, there would be a number of houses without a complete roof tomorrow.

At midnight Cap Jim, Gerald, Durgan, Quimby, and others were heard coming in the store. At first, from the voices and the noise, Steven thought they had returned with sailors from the wreck. Then he made out that the wind and the rain had been too much for their efforts, and they had abandoned them. They had brought back one of the kegs. Steven heard the blow that broached it and then the tinkle of glasses being passed out.

Drinking and singing, they rode the storm and the night through. Steven, kept awake by the noise, listened to the wind. For another hour it kept up, but grew no stronger. Then, gradually, it began to slacken and its force to abate. This could be noted first by its change of direction. The palms on the south side of the store now thrashed no more violently than those on the north. The sounds evened out, to show that the wind was coming from nearly due east. This meant that the hurricane was moving north out at sea.

The roistering men in the store noted it, too, for Cap Jim roared for silence. They listened, and in a moment there came the joyful call, "It's going on past! It ain't going to hit us!" They cheered, while Doc called vainly for them to stop their racket.

The hilarity of the all-night celebrants was subdued for a time when the party of some twenty men went to the beach at dawn. Although the force of the gale had dropped, the sea itself had lost none of its wild activity. On it could be seen no ship. No expected wreckage or the bodies of sailors had washed up. There were only the kegs, dotting the shore in both directions. Others bobbed in the surf, the sea playing with them before finally relinquishing them.

Some of the men had provided themselves with hammers and hatchets for bungstarters. A few carried pegs with which to seal up the casks after they had been opened and tested. Cap Jim, who organized the work, delegated the older men to start on the kegs within a mile on either side of where they stood. Others he sent farther off in both directions. The main body of searchers, headed by himself, would go north to where most of the booty had washed.

"You'll come with us," he told the Deacon. As if by pre-arrangement, he took one of the Deacon's arms, and Dewey Durgan, happily staggering, took the other. The Deacon looked uncertain, but had little chance to express his feelings as he was marched off.

Steven and Quimby, as the best beach walkists, were to go as far south as the last keg, and work back from there. They now set out, passing other men already at work. The stronger men lifted the casks high in the air and put their mouths to them to taste. Sometimes they smacked their lips and handed the keg gently to those waiting above on the sand bank to receive it. More frequently they spat and disgustedly threw the keg back into the sea, letting it roll out again to be grasped by the water, the wine running like blood in the white foam.

"I never had much experience at this," Steven told Quimby.

"I didn't have any, either, till last night," Quimby answered. His nearly white hair blew into his flushed face. "You get on to it easy."

Quimby pronounced good the first keg they tested, and handed it to Steven for his verdict. Holding it with both hands above his head, Steven tried to duplicate Quimby's feat of putting his mouth to the bunghole before the wine spilled out. He failed, and the liquid splashed across his face. Then his mouth filled with a rush, and he could taste the sharp sherry. The wine kept coming and he had to swallow to make room for it.

When he put down the keg he choked and blinked. His throat burned. But in his stomach a pleasant warmth spread.

Quimby, watching his face, said, "That's what I meant."

It was surprising to discover how many of the casks were spoiled, and just as astonishing to learn how much testing the others required before being found good. In the process Steven didn't remember when he lost Quimby.

Whether they took different directions in the morning, or in the afternoon, was open to some question. Just what time of day it was could be a matter for a good deal of debate. The sky still scudded with close, gray clouds, and the light had been the same all day. Putting it up to himself, Steven decided he didn't care about that or about Quimby. He felt too fine to care much about anything.

Never before had he known such an exhilaration. His limbs were loose and carefree. They seemed extraordinarily light, as if they had lost a good deal of weight. Little effort was required to move them. His arms swung with abandon, his feet lifted of themselves and were put down as though they walked on air.

He felt very sure of himself. He was certain that if Adie were only here he could tell her anything he cared to. Nothing could hold him back.

Suddenly he wanted her to be here and his regret that she wasn't struck him forcibly.

He came upon Cap Jim sprawled on his back, his legs wide apart, his arms flung out in a supplicating gesture, his beard pointing at the sky. Snuggled on one side of him was Gerald, whose head rested comfortably on one of the greater man's shoulders. On the other side was Durgan, snoring and puffing. All three looked quite comfortable.

Then Steven didn't care about them any more. The thought of Adie came to him again. It made him feel lonely. He started back for the store.

On the path he nearly stumbled over the Deacon, who lay there, a silly smile on his face, which worked spasmodically. His eyes were closed. There was no doubt about his condition.

Methodically, Steven lifted the slight body to his shoulder. He plodded along with it, reaching the Thomas House to find Mrs. Thomas standing on the porch. Her hand went to her throat and then came away again. Her lips pressed together. She told Steven:

"Poor dear man. He was so anxious to help. The work must have been too much for him. His good will and honorable purpose were overcome. But who is there to blame him when it was all for a good cause?"

Steven didn't blame him. Weaving on his feet, he simply wanted to get rid of the Deacon.

Mrs. Thomas motioned for him to bring her husband inside. She led the way to one of the chambers. Steven dumped the Deacon on the bed and then obeyed when Mrs. Thomas commanded him to help her. She pulled off the Deacon's shoes while Steven fumbled with his coat. She took over the work on the Deacon's shirt when he got nowhere with it.

Steven stood watching. Through his fascination there began to creep slow horror. The woman seemed to have forgotten his presence.

The Deacon appeared in his long underwear. Mrs. Thomas worked at the chest buttons, and then the Deacon himself began to emerge.

Blindly, Steven fled.

He made his way to the store and to his room. Here his eye caught the nautilus. Once more Adie came to him. He picked up the shell and looked at it. Abruptly, his fingers seemed to turn to jelly and he dropped it.

There was a tinkling crash, and the shell lay in a thousand pieces on the floor.

Then Steven knew how drunk he was himself.

Eighteen

Doc HAD TO GET HIM UP in the morning and start him on his way. He stood by Steven's bed snapping his armbands, pushing out his lips, and peering over his spectacles all at the same time while he lectured, "Yesterday will be a day long remembered with shame in this community. I hauled practically the entire male population home. Let me tell you it wasn't easy getting things straightened out in some houses."

Steven groaned.

Doc's feet crunched on the remains of the nautilus. He looked down at it and said, "There's another thing to show you what drink can do. I only hope that this is the end for you, Stevie, instead of the beginning."

"If it makes you feel the way I do," Steven told him, "you ain't got a thing to worry about."

"So you'll be sure of that, I won't give you any medicine for it, even though I got a good one." Then, solicitously, Doc inquired, "Head bad?"

"A bomb just went off inside it."

"Mouth bad?"

"I ain't got a tongue, but a piece of felt."

Doc steeled himself. "That's good. I'll fix you some breakfast—"

"Not for me you won't," Steven said with finality.

His haversack was like a hundredweight on his back that day. Wobbly on his legs, he couldn't keep to his accustomed gait, so that the walking tired him twice as much as usual. Ordinarily he would have been concerned with what had happened to the beach in the blow. Today he didn't care. He barely noted how much more sand had been sucked out by its perennial enemy. He didn't stop to figure how long it would be before the beach would fill in again, the sea in its own time, when through with what it had stolen, returning it. He didn't even want to waste any energy in going over to Hypoluxo to see if there had been damage there.

The wind kept up, dropped from a gale to a steady, hard breeze. The sea itself was still filled with anger, and would remain so for some days. The sun was out, streaming down on him in the humid air. His body became soaked with sweat. He felt feverish. In his weakened condition, he stumbled. He plodded on through the day.

By the time he arrived at the house of refuge, the earth was rising and sinking before Steven's eyes, heaving dizzily. The Pagets looked at him in wonder when he shuffled in. Linda observed, "You got the fair look of a dog walkin' with his tail between his legs."

Rocking on his feet, Steven told them about the great wine wreck. The effects of that, together with the walking in the sun today, had been a little too much for him. "You look at me," he mumbled, "and you don't see a human being, but something crawling under a palmetto."

Jesse said something about heatstroke. Della mentioned food. Steven waved this aside and made his way to the stairs leading to the loft. "I just need to sleep," he said.

Jesse followed him up and helped him out of his clothes and into bed. Steven lay gratefully. He was spent. "Wake me at daybreak," he murmured.

" 'The mail must go,' " Jesse quoted. He added ironically, "Even if it kills somebody."

"You wake me," Steven told him.

"Not a minute late," Jesse assured him.

Steven thought that Jesse's tone was peculiar. He tried to concentrate on it, but sleep drew him too strongly.

The sun was high when Steven awakened by himself. He still felt a little shaky, but enormously refreshed. He sat up, alarmed. Jesse hadn't kept his word. He would be late getting the mail into Miami.

He jumped off the cot. In the middle of pulling on his clothes he noticed that his haversack was missing from the spot on the floor where he had dropped it the previous night. He looked around. It was nowhere to be seen.

He got into his clothes fast, then, and clattered down the stairs.

Linda and Della were sitting in the living room. He asked, "What's happened?" He stared about. "Where's Jesse?"

Linda gazed at him with disapproval. She glanced at Della and said, "You tell him."

Della explained, "Jesse took the mail for you. He didn't think you should go, feeling the way you did."

Instantly, Steven thought of the beachcombers. He strode to the door to look at the day and judge the time. He saw it was well toward noon. He went back into the room slowly.

"He said," Della told him, "you weren't to follow after, even if you woke in time."

"It's past time," Steven said, "and he shouldn't have done it."

"You're to look after us," Della said. She turned to him, moving her heavy body awkwardly. "Steven, he's been wanting to get down to Miami to have a look at what Sylvanus Hurley is doing." Della laughed, the way she laughed with Jesse. "He also said he has to meet Adie sometime, and now is as good a time as any. He'll ask her to marry you, since you can't do it yourself."

"Joking about Jesse's goin'," Linda said, "makes it worse." The old lady had been looking blackly at her daughter-in-law.

"It's bad luck fer a man to leave his wife when she's goin' to have birth."

Della shook her head. "It isn't for another five weeks."

"Jesse Paget," Linda predicted, "is astin' fer trouble, an' he's goin' to git it."

Steven didn't mention his own fears, not wanting to upset Della with them. They might be groundless in any case. He said, "Jesse's traveled the route more times than me."

"Nothin' good will come of it," Linda told them both. "You mark my words."

Alternately, during the next four days, Linda scolded or lapsed into a wordless conviction that something was going to happen to Jesse. She blamed Della for letting him go. She blamed Steven for being the cause of his going. Steven began to feel guilty until he saw that Della, with a new kind of inner peace she had found during the recent weeks, had learned not to be disturbed by the old lady. Then he followed suit, humoring Linda while at the same time wondering how Jesse was making out.

He told himself there was no cause for worry, that Jesse would be back Friday afternoon on schedule. He told himself that the beachcombers would not attack him, certainly not beyond robbing the mail again. Steven didn't like to think of them, but he couldn't credit any real threat there.

For Della he picked the small bananas which grew back of the orange grove; she seemed to have an insatiable appetite for them, a continuous craving. Of this Linda observed, "I had a love fer guavas afore Jesse come." She spoke as if this were a better choice.

The old lady busied herself at making candles and soap, with Steven glad to assist her to take up his time. It was not necessary for the Pagets to home-manufacture either, but Linda insisted that hers were better than the store-bought varieties. She boiled bayberries until the wax rose to the top, thick and gray, and then skimmed it off to roll it by hand around manila cords for the wicks.

Linda worked Steven hard at making alligator soap. He had to go deep in the scrub with a machete to cut mastic. In the rear of the house, partially out of the wind, he made great bonfires of the wood. The ashes were put into a barrel set a foot from the ground on three legs, and over it was poured fresh water. In a pail below, the lye was caught as the mixture worked and dropped out a hole made for it. Placed in a kettle under which another fire was built, Linda then threw in the clear white fat of an alligator Jesse had killed. This finally set into a hard coarse soap Della refused to use. Linda declared it was the best anybody could make, and that Della showed her Cuban ignorance by turning up her nose at it.

On Friday afternoon they watched, from the porch steps, for Jesse to return. They peered down the beach, expecting to see him any minute. Slowly the afternoon passed and he didn't come. Linda gave up the vigil and went to her room, saying, "Watchin' fer him keeps him away."

Steven and Della kept at their post. Steven agreed with her that there was no reason to expect trouble, that the old lady merely made them nervous with her superstitious predictions, and that they had started to wait for Jesse too soon. He might not arrive until evening.

Still they remained to watch, anxious for the sight of him.

A ship, hugging the shore less than half a mile out to escape running against the flow of the Stream, came south. Steven recognized it as the Lampasas of the Mallory Line, bound for Key West. He went inside to record the time of its passing in the station's log. When he came out again, Della shook her head before he could look down the beach to see nothing there in the descending night.

At supper, Steven and Della one minute believed their assurances to each other that nothing had happened to Jesse, that he was simply late after probably not getting started from Miami in time two days ago. The next minute they didn't believe them. Linda helped not at all by saying, "It's come, jist like I said. He won't git here at all."

Steven, on edge from the waiting and his own secret fears, told her, "Stop saying that."

"I kin say it if I want," Linda replied pettishly.

"You can't know it," Della told her quietly.

"I do know it!" Linda said like a cross child. "I kin feel it. I felt it from the first."

Steven thought of setting out to meet Jesse. That was the way he expressed it and tried to have faith in it. The two women told him what he knew already. If something had actually happened to Jesse, he might miss him on the beach. Steven reflected that he should have started after him four days ago.

Linda didn't sit up. She said there was no need. There was nothing to wait for. "Jesse ain't goin' to git here. Never agin."

Della had a frightened look on her face while Steven waited with her until late. They spoke little, listening for every sound in the night. Della was pale, and once she showed evidences of pain inside her swollen body that made Steven so alarmed he ordered her to go to bed. At first she refused. Then she got up without a word and made her way to her chamber as if walking in her sleep.

Finally, Steven went himself to one of the cots in the loft. He lay there still listening and hearing nothing except the wind and the lessening pound of the breakers on the beach. He refused to accept that there was anything wrong. Jesse had made the same trip, all the way from Jupiter, a hundred times. He knew every inch of the way and all the conditions. The rivers, even in flood, should give him no trouble. He could take care of himself in all ways.

Something else had occurred, something with no dread or danger in it. Maybe the keeper at the Lauderdale house of refuge was sick and Jesse had stayed to help him. That was as good an explanation as any. Jesse would arrive to laugh at their fears.

Conscious of the two women downstairs who waited and listened, too, Steven remained tense and alert. His heart sank when he could perceive the light of dawn coming up the stair way and there had been no sign of Jesse.

Nineteen

STANDING IN HER BARE FEET, Linda pinned up her skirts so that they reached only to her spindly shins. On her head she wore a palmetto hat tied with a string under her chin. Watching her, Della sat with her hands placed over her great stomach as if caressing and reassuring the new life there.

Steven asked Linda, "What do you think you're fixing to do?"

"I'm goin' with you," she answered.

"You ain't. Not two steps."

Linda went on with the work at her skirts. "Jesse's dead," she said.

Steven glanced at Della. She paid no attention.

"Do you think I ain't goin' to find him?" Linda demanded.

He told her, "You can't last walking the beach."

"You don't have the knowin' of how I kin do. You young folks got the new idea of what life is like, an' it's different from what it was in my time. I'm goin', an' you can't put a stop to me."

"I tell you you'll hold me up."

"Iffen I do," she replied sharply, "you keep right on. I'll git there, an' mebbe ahead of you."

Steven offered what he thought was a greater objection. "You can't leave Della here alone."

"I'll be all right," Della said. She lifted large eyes that stared like those of some hurt, uncomprehending animal.

Steven still fought with the old lady. "You can't do any good. There's no reason for you to go."

Linda, finished with the work on her skirts, stood straight. "I got flesh out there callin' me. It's mine, right from me, same as hers is comin' soon from her. I hear it. I feel it. I got to go to it."

Steven said to Della. "I'll make her stay if you say so."

She turned her head slowly from side to side.

"You ready?" Linda demanded. She started briskly out of the house, not waiting for him.

His anger rising, Steven called after her in a last desperate attempt to stop her. "You damned old woman!"

She heard, but kept on her way without hesitation or reply.

Steven stood for a moment, then mounted the stairs two at a time to the loft. He threw off his shoes and socks and yanked up his trousers. Then he went to the government stores piled at the far end. Taking up a package of biscuits he broke it open. He stuffed his pockets full, found his cap, and went downstairs again. In the kitchen he snatched a tin cup, unbuckled his belt and slipped the handle of the cup in the strap so that it dangled at his waist.

In the living room Della sat as before, staring straight in front of her, blankly, without expression. Steven wondered if she saw him. He had meant to tell her that they would hurry, or that he would send Linda back, but now he could find no way to address her. He went after the old lady.

She was well down the beach. He had nearly to run to catch up with her. When he reached her he said, "You can't go on this fast. Slow down if you want to get anywhere."

She didn't answer. Beneath the wide brim of her hat, her thin lined face was set and grim, her eyes beady and blazing with determination. She refused to follow his advice, and kept on as she had started out.

Though the wind continued to blow, the sea had calmed. The half tide, coming in, gave them room to walk between the water and the high scarp. Steven headed the way, leading the old lady over the hardest surface, avoiding for her sake the white shell patches marking ground that would hold them up and take a little more energy.

She appeared to mind nothing. She didn't slow the pace, she showed no sign of faltering. She refused to act upon any suggestion to stop and rest. Steven couldn't fathom how she did it, from where she obtained the strength. It could hardly be in her frail limbs. It seemed to come from elsewhere, from a secret, veiled source.

They watched for some sign of Jesse's passing. The tides since he came this way had washed to oblivion all imprints of his footsteps. But there might be something else. There might be Jesse himself.

They found nothing until they reached the Boca Raton rocks jutting out fifty feet into the sea eight miles below the house of refuge. Here the sand bank was broken, showing where Jesse had climbed it. Marks of his feet in the narrow beach plain above led across and into the scrub. There were no marks to be seen showing his return, and that frightened Steven.

Curiously, Linda wasn't disturbed by the one-way trail and didn't want to follow it. "That ain't where he is," she declared. "You kin look, but we got to go on to find him."

He left her sitting on the sand, finally resting, while he made his way along Jesse's path. He had to guess at it through the tangled mass of Spanish bayonet. He came out at the right place on the shore of Boca Raton Lake. In the marl he could make out the imprint of Jesse's feet where he had waded out to get a drink in the clear fresh water. There were, again, no footprints to show that he had come back.

Steven acted out Jesse's movements as best he could, to follow them. As he dipped his tin cup and drank he didn't want to look in the water for fear of what he might see. He forced himself to search, but there was nothing to discover of Jesse. A flight of curlew skimmed close over the surface on the far side of the lake, each ibis a white dot pricking the green background. Steven looked for a telltale buzzard that might be hovering over the shoreline. There was none.

He filled the cup for Linda and then searched for Jesse's way back to the beach, if there had been any way. Fifty feet down the lake shore he found it. Jesse had waded in the water to here, and returned to the beach by another route through the scrub.

Guessing again, Steven came out somewhat below where he had entered the undergrowth. This time he missed the trail by several yards. But the footprints led back to the sand bank, down it, and then presumably on.

Linda, watching for him, joined Steven at the edge of the surf. She drank the water he brought for her, and then waited no longer before going on.

Four miles ahead lay the jutting point of land made by Hillsborough. Soon it could be made out clearly. As they approached, Steven squinted tightly to catch a glimpse of anything that might indicate Jesse's story. At first he wasn't sure of what he saw, and dreaded recognizing it.

Off the mouth of the river black fins showed leisurely, deliberately, thrust above the surface of the water. They came up, to appear and tell of to what they were attached below. Then they sank, until, a moment later, they were to be seen again.

There were not just a few sharks, as usual, waiting off the inlet for whatever might come out, or darting in on quick, vicious forays to search. There were hundreds of them dotting the water, the fins streaking in a wide area to show a congress of the creatures.

Steven told himself it didn't have to mean anything in connection with Jesse. By itself it probably didn't. In its implications Linda now, with her remark, showed that it could.

"Don't need to think I fail to see it," she sniffed. "Them critters mean somethin' ain't natural up there."

They heard it before they saw it. Even above the wind they caught the bellowing, the grunting, and the sound of splashing and fighting.

"Gators," said Linda. She sounded as if she had expected to hear them.

They reached a point from where they could glimpse the inlet through the trees. "More gators," Steven said awesomely, "than you or anybody else has ever seen before."

The bar at the mouth of the inlet had been completely altered by the blow since Steven passed here. The waves, in building it up instead of taking it away, had gone further, and made a complete dam of it, caging the river. The water, flowing down strongly from the torrential rains, was piling up many feet above the ocean level. The stream had overflowed its banks, so that the banyans as well as the cypresses stood with their feet covered by it. In places Spanish moss touched the surface, its ends dragging in the current.

All about was the destruction the storm had caused in the dense growth. Lianas were twisted in new positions where they did not grow but were thrust; fallen air plants littered the ground; great masses of mangrove roots were added to the dead wood now piled in windrows; here and there an orchid lay crushed, or torn from its perch to be given another.

At the dam which closed the inlet, the water was alive with thousands of fish. Trapped in the river when they came from the ocean at high tide to feed, they now wished for the sea again. They clung, packed nearly solid, to the edge of the dam, gasping for what salt water seeped through.

This was the merest part of their travail. In the new lagoon they occupied were dozens of alligators. News of the feast had gone far up the Hillsborough. Steven revised his first estimate. There were more gators than he thought ever existed. "Look!" he cried to Linda, quite as if she did not have eyes herself to see.

Fourteen-foot gator chased ten-foot and ten-foot charged after eight-foot in savage pursuit of the fish. Sometimes part of the imprisoned school, frantic with the combined desire for the sea and to get away from their attackers, left the bar and darted part way back up the river. A phalanx of alligators, swift under the water, went after them. Out of the swirls and splashings what remained of the fish afterward made their way back to the bar, pushing against those ahead. The fish leaped sometimes up on the sand, in an effort to get away or jump the barrier. There many of them flopped and many more lay dead. The stench from these permeated the air.

From the bull gators there came deep, ground-shaking bellows and grunts. From the females there were hisses, sibilant to show them for the reptiles they were. Great roars and the sound of snapping jaws rose from a number of fights among themselves. One would get another by a short stubby leg, and hold on while they thrashed together, rolling over and over, frothing the water and staining it as the limb was wrenched off. A penetrating odor of musk mixed with that of decaying fish.

It was this savage slaughter that the sharks sensed. They waited on it, swimming slowly up and down beyond the bar. Patiently, they patrolled for the moment they might be able to join the battle. And it seemed that moment was not far off, for the water of the river was piling up fast against the dam, soon to slop over. And the sea itself was now also rising to eat at its base, ready to destroy what it had constructed.

Linda was the first to tear herself away from the sight. It was Steven who followed her as she began to search along the shore of the river for some further sign of Jesse. She told Steven above the noise from the lagoon, "The gators got him. They ate him."

Steven, though it was with a sinking sensation, wasn't yet ready to admit this. If the boat was gone it meant that Jesse might be somewhere farther on down the beach, and safe.

He made his way to the place where he had drawn up the

boat and secreted it. The air-root of the banyan to which he had tied it led a foot down in the water where before it had been on land. There were still faint marks on it where the rope had been secured. The boat itself was not in sight, nor could he see it on the other side of the flooded stream.

But when he informed Linda of this, wanting to give her hope, she answered, "Can't you know yit he's gone, that them things got him in their bellies? Can't you see what I got in my hands, an' what's hangin' on that bush?"

He stared at her. He hadn't noticed that she held a small pile of clothes. He recognized them at once for Jesse's. He turned to the bush she indicated.

There, fastened to a branch, was his haversack.

Slowly he went to it. His hands, almost apart from himself, lifted up the flap, and he looked inside. The mail bag was there, along with the other contents. Nothing was missing. There was no note from Jesse telling what he had done.

Steven needed none. He saw it as if it were he instead of Jesse—as it should have been. The boat wasn't there when Jesse searched for it. The beachcombers, choosing this moment, selecting another by mistake upon whom to take their revenge, had removed it. The dam, when Jesse arrived five days ago, hadn't yet formed; he couldn't cross by that. The river simply swelled in flood, with some of the gators and an occasional shark busy in it. In spite of them, Jesse had stripped and started swimming across, hoping to find the boat on the other side and return to get his clothes and the mail.

Steven didn't like to believe that anything in the water had killed him. He preferred to think that Jesse had been swept out to sea and drowned.

The first wave of his being responsible for Jesse's death engulfed him. He could feel his face twitching as he turned to Linda.

"You got no call to look like that," she told him. "He was bound to go. Nothin' could stop him."

In a low voice, hoarse from his constricted throat, he reminded, "You said yourself I was to blame."

"You got to git over thinkin' like that, in a quick hurry," she said sharply. "You didn't ast him to do it. He offered. It was his own doin'."

Steven thanked her with his eyes. But it didn't take away all of his guilt, and it didn't bring Jesse back. They stood there looking at each other helplessly.

Linda held her head to one side, in a listening attitude. "You hear it?" she asked.

Steven thought she must be affected by Jesse's death. She had been uncanny before in predicting and knowing what had happened; now her mind might be touched.

Then he heard it himself. It sounded like a wail, yet could be recognized for a voice calling from across the river. It was a woman's voice. Something familiar in it made his heart jump.

When they walked to a more open space at the stream's shore, Steven had a second shock. Seen through a curtain of vines on the other side was Adie.

She waved and called again. Steven could think of but one thing to yell against the wind: "What are you doing here?"

Her answer, if she heard him at all to reply, was carried away by the wind. He called once more, and this time she made motions, pointing upstream, and indicating to him to follow her up on his side.

He obeyed, flinging back to Linda words to tell her who Adie was. He was alarmed and distracted by her appearance. Clad in a pinned-up dress like Linda, her hair was bound tightly in braids about her head. This meant that as a woman this time she had risked the trip along the beach alone.

When Adie stopped and he arrived opposite her, they were farther away from each other than before at a widening of the river. At her feet he saw the boat. That was what she meant.

Now she made preparations to launch it and come across. At her action Steven yelled for her to stop. She couldn't have seen what was happening at the mouth of the river or understood the noises or smells coming from there.

She failed to hear him warn her now that if she crossed in the boat when the bar gave way she would be drawn out to the sharks and among the alligators. Steven screamed and gesticulated, but she looked at him without comprehension. She seemed moved by some insistent desire to get across as she struggled with getting the boat into the water.

Steven turned and ran to the ocean. He passed Linda standing with something new in her hands. He didn't notice what it was as he rushed past her. Streaking as fast as his legs would carry him, he reached the tongue of land holding back the river.

The water had reached within a few inches of the top. On the other side small landslides occurred when the sea there tugged at it. There was only a narrow path across the top over which to cross.

He started. He didn't get the stench in his nostrils, nor was he conscious of the packed, struggling fish his flying feet nearly touched, and he didn't see the cavernous jaws not much farther away. His weight was held only because of his pace. Once his foot went down, deep in the sand, and was instantly washed by an eager stream spurting from the lagoon. He started the first opening, which widened even as he crossed.

On the other side he fought his way through a tangle of growth, pull-and-haul-back vines yanking at his clothes and tearing his flesh. He stumbled, fell, rose, and pushed his way on. He didn't know he was yelling.

He arrived to find that Adie had the boat launched from the bank and was about to get in. He grabbed her by the wrist. Breathless, he stared at her. She gazed back, and all at once he saw that she was as driven with emotion as he, and the more so at his sudden wild appearance.

Before they could speak, there came the sound of a roaring of water. It grew in volume. Still holding Adie's wrist, Steven led her back to the beach.

She gasped at what was to be seen there. The break in the dam had now widened to some yards. Water poured through it powerfully, filled with fish. One of the alligators was carried through, feet kicking and tail lashing. Even as they watched, the bar gave way in another place close by the first opening. A second later the sand between the two collapsed, and then the whole contents of the lagoon was being swept into the ocean.

A cascade of fish and alligators went out in a fighting, tangled melée. White, hard-scaled broad under sides were turned to the sky. Once a writhing tail slapped a jumping fish and sent it yards over the water.

The sharks met them hardly a dozen yards from shore. The water became blood as shark sliced open gator belly and gator ripped open shark, and the fish darted in and about, under and above, the two. Something only half there clawed its way out and collapsed on the sand as the red stream of the battle began to run far into the sea.

Twenty

A SHAKEN ADIE explained her presence as Steven rowed the boat across the river. The further effects of the low pressure brought by the threatened hurricane had taken her mother near to death. The tonic alone seemed to keep her alive, and though she was somewhat improved now, she still needed it. Then, accidentally, Adie dropped the bottle, breaking it.

No boat would put out to go to Palm Beach to get another. Adie waited for Steven to come, so that he could bring a new supply on his next trip. When he didn't arrive, she set out by herself. She hadn't seen the beachcombers. The boat at New River had also been taken to the south side, and she used it to cross and stay last night at the Lauderdale house of refuge.

Steven cursed the keeper for not accompanying her the rest of the way. He growled, "Wasn't there anybody else in Miami to make the trip?"

She told him there had been a good deal of storm damage. Many of the tents blew away, parts of other houses had gone. People had their own troubles to attend to. "Our thatch was torn off," she said. "It was raining and father had to stay to fix the roof."

Steven made no bones about his next question. "How about Sylvanus?"

She looked away, up the river. "He was in Key West, on business—and the mail schooner waited out the hurricane there."

Linda was at the shore to meet them. Steven helped Adie out of the boat and made the old lady known to her. He was watching Adie while he spoke, beginning to explain Linda's presence and Jesse having started on the trip for him. Suddenly he saw Adie's face become ashen. She took in her breath sharply.

Then Steven saw what Linda held in her hands. Tenderly she carried a piece of torn flesh to which broken ribs were attached.

"I found him on the shore," the old lady said simply. "He ain't no much more than a piece of sidemeat, but that part of him got away from them."

Steven, his stomach turning over, couldn't stand the sight of it. He glanced about, saw the clothes Linda had put down. Striding to them he snatched at them and brought them back. Thrusting them at Linda, he told her in a strained voice, "Cover it up. Get it out of sight."

Linda wrapped in Jesse's clothes what she held. "I birthed

him," she murmured. "An' when his flesh is near mine I kin tell it. There ain't a lot to bury. But that's what I come for. To take back what there is."

Adie recovered. She found her voice. She seemed to realize, intuitively, many things about Linda. Softly, she suggested, "Wouldn't it be better to bury him here?"

Linda stared at her bundle. "He'd like it most iffen he was took home."

"You ain't going to carry that—" Steven began, and then stopped when Adie shook her head at him.

"Let her," she said.

They started out, Linda leading the way with her terrible burden.

Mostly they walked silently. The old lady kept up, her spirit instead of her strength carrying her along. What hunger they had was met with the biscuits in Steven's pockets. They stopped to drink of Boca Raton water, and then continued.

Steven caught up with Adie and walked by her side. Somberly, he told her about the wine wreck and just why Jesse had taken his place. Ahead, Linda said nothing, and Adie did not comment until they had made their way on for another twenty yards. Then she put her hand on his arm for an instant and said, "Your part of it was an accident."

He dropped back, to thank her with his gaze for her absolution. But it wasn't complete, and he felt only a preliminary adjustment, tentative and unsatisfactory, about Jesse.

They reached the house of refuge in the early evening when it was still light. Steven approached with dread. From the porch, after they entered, he saw Della sitting in the same chair where he left her that morning. She might not have moved.

Blocking the doorway, Steven turned to Linda and whispered, "Leave it out here."

Linda hesitated. She acted as if she were not going to obey, until Adie touched her shoulder. Then she looked about and saw a small wood goods box on the floor near the wall. "Right here is about the size for his coffin," she said. She went to the box and put the bundle in it.

Della was on her feet when they went in. Her eyes were larger than ever. Slowly they went from one to the other of them, resting on Adie for a brief moment before going back to Steven and Linda. She didn't need to be told what had happened.

Linda was the first to speak, shrilly, in a way that emphasized the manner she had always treated Della. "It's what come from the Cuban part of him," she told her. "Jist like his pa. An' it's what come of him bein' married to a Cuban," she accused.

The peace Della had found with the old lady, already drained away, was now joined by the fear she had borne for the last twenty-four hours. Goaded beyond endurance, she broke. Crying hysterical, unintelligible imprecations, she flung herself at Linda. Her fists came up to flail at her, beating, and beating again.

Linda stood still, receiving the blows without protest or voluntary movement. When she was thrust off balance, she braced herself to remain firm to invite more of the punishment. On her face was all her bitterness, all her sorrow, and the last of her hate for Della.

Linda's hat, torn from her head by Della's attack, fell to the floor. At the sight of it dropping down, Della stopped. She stared at the old lady as if seeing her for the first time. In their gaze there seemed to be the mutual understanding that now they were both without Jesse, that neither of them could have him ever again, that all they had was each other and the promise, to be shared, of what lay within one of them. In that moment the acid of their entire previous relationship was expended.

Sobbing, Della fell against Linda. The old lady took her in her arms. As the sobs came stronger, Linda patted her, stroking her head and soothing her.

They parted when Della went stiff with pain. She clutched at her stomach, writhing.

Linda gazed at her contortions, evaluating them. "It's coming ahead of its time," she said. She pulled up a chair and placed Della's hands on its back. "Hang on to that till it's over," she advised.

The old lady turned to Steven and Adie, who had stood, held by what passed between the two women, powerless to interfere.

"You ever bin at a birth?" Linda asked Adie.

She shook her head. She was white, but resolute.

"Think you kin help?" Linda wanted to know.

"I'll try," Adie whispered. "I'll do what I can."

"Didn't I heer you say you got a ma who needs medicine bad?" Linda asked.

"I'll stay here," Adie told her. "As long as you want me to."

Gimlet eyes gave their approval. They fastened on Steven. "Git the fire goin' in the stove," the old lady instructed. "Put on every kittle we got, full of water, an' keep it boilin'."

It was hours since Linda and Adie took Della into her bedroom. For most of the time Steven had kept the kitchen stove red. Great clouds of steam rose from the kettles. The house became hot, nearly stifling. Linda stuck her head out of the bedroom door and admonished him, "There wasn't nothin' I said about burnin' the place down."

He cut off the draft a little, yet didn't dare let the fire get too low for fear the water might not be right.

Once Adie came out to get toweling and cloths. Steven had to show her where they were kept. Another time she came out for, perversely, a basin of cold water. They had used none of the hot except for a small pitcher he took to them, passing it inside.

Adie said nothing about how things were going. She kept to her duties. She wore a white apron over her dress, and her sleeves were rolled to the elbow. She looked tense and a little drawn.

Steven thought it must be over by now. From Della had come, for some time, great long groans, sometimes sharp cries. She would be silent for a while, and then the groans and cries would come again. The intervals between them became less frequent. He could hear movements in the bedroom, occasionally the sound of footsteps like those of a person pacing. He wondered what that was for.

Seated on a hard wooden chair in the kitchen, he dozed. He would come fully awake only when there was a noise from the bedroom. He waited, to see if they wanted anything. Then he dozed again, and finally slept.

He came to as an ear-splitting scream sent itself through the house. He sat bolt upright, and then got to his feet. The scream came again.

He left the kitchen, rushing to the bedroom door. When he reached there, he stopped, looking at the blank door. From behind it the scream came a third time. No one came out. He could hear the mumble of Linda's voice, that of Adie answering. The screams kept coming faster.

Steven left the door, and wandered around the living room. He turned up the wick of the lamp which was flickering. He went back to the kitchen. Della's agony reached him there as well. She sounded like some animal being tortured.

Steven looked at the stove, to see that the redness had left it. Alarmed, he piled in wood until the iron glowed again. Then he adjusted the draft and left the house. The women would have their water, could call if they needed him.

The clouds had finally cleared from the sky. Straight above, a quarter moon shone, lighting the sea and the earth. He was surprised to see it so high.

He decided that Della, because the birth was premature, must be dying. Maybe it would be a good thing. If the child lived, he and Adie would take it. They would raise it with their own. He realized to what lengths his morbid and fantastic imagination was leading him. Della screeched in agony.

Suddenly he wanted to be doing something. He knew at once what it was to be. He went around the house, to the back. There he found a shovel. He carried it away from the house. Della's cries still reached him, but didn't seem so bad now that he occupied himself.

When he came to the top of the low ridge overlooking the sea he was sure that this would be Jesse's own choice. He began to dig. At first his muscles trembled, and he could barely get the shovel into the soft white sand. After a moment they steadied and his movements became methodical, his mind alone racing with the realization of what he was doing.

It didn't have to be deep. The box wasn't very large, and inside the box there was very little of Jesse. Now Steven was glad Linda had brought it. It wouldn't have seemed right to leave any part of Jesse without bringing him home and giving him a burial.

The dry top sand flowed back into the hole, and it was some time before he reached the more solid, damp sand below. This held, so that the square he took out of the earth grew until he judged it was large enough.

The screams from the house had stopped. He hadn't been conscious of when they were to be heard no more.

Dropping the shovel, he went back. No one was in the living room. No sound came from the bedroom. He looked into the kitchen, and saw that several of the kettles had been removed from the stove. He returned to the living room to hear Linda and Adie speaking in low voices.

Abruptly, another sound came. It was a thin, ragged wail. A baby cried for the first time, protesting its entrance into a new, strange world.

The partial relief from the well of dread that had gripped Steven ever since he and Linda arrived at Hillsborough stimulated him to using his hands again. In addition, he wanted to have Jesse's burial ready, with no more action from Linda. He went out through the rear entrance of the house and there, in the shed, found boards, a saw, a hammer and nails. Carrying these he took them to the porch. He forced himself to measure, to saw, and finally to nail.

As he finished, he heard the bedroom door open. He sprang up and went inside.

Adie came out. She carried, carefully in both arms, a bundle wrapped in a piece of torn blanket.

She motioned to Steven. He went over to her. With one finger she pulled the blanket a little away, and he looked down at a tiny red wrinkled face, screwed tightly in sleep.

"It's a boy," Adie said. She looked at Steven and in her words there was understanding of most things he felt. "It's Jesse."

Steven thought of the other Jesse. He had been so sure it would be a boy. And now it was. And now he wasn't here to see and laugh and boast.

Steven regretted, deeply and passionately, that it had not been him instead of Jesse. His self-accusation was bitter and cutting. He resolved that if it would give Jesse any reason or honor for dying, he would never take a drink again as long as he lived.

If Adie had been through a trying experience, she didn't show it. Her face was no longer tense or drawn. Relaxed, there shone from it a tenderness and an exaltation. Her gray eyes were lighted with pride. She exhibited, as a woman, the unequaled fruit of all women. The child in her arms rested comfortably, content and at home.

Adie could even smile at the concern she saw on Steven's face when he looked toward the closed door of the bedroom. "Della's all right," she said. She looked down at the child. "She'll be—she'll have him."

Adie went back to the bedroom.

It was dawn when both she and Linda came out again. The old lady, her shoulders still straight, walked to the porch, and

Steven and Adie followed her out. She sat in her shoofly chair. Automatically, she began to pedal it. The fringe went back and forth slowly, touching her face lightly. As if she realized what she was doing, she stopped. She sighed, looked about, and saw the box. She stared at it for a moment before she said:

"I see you got it fixed. I heered you gittin' the shovel, too. I'd like to of had a regular box for him. I'd like to of had a good preacher. But mebbe nothin' atall is better than the best we could git from upcountry, sich as one of these here tent lizards. Or that Deacon from the lake." She paused. "We best git on with it. We got one borned. The other is past ready to go back."

Steven carried the box ahead of them to the ridge. He deposited it gently in the shallow grave. Linda took up a handful of sand and stepping forward, let it trickle through her fingers on the box. Hesitantly, then surely, Adie followed the custom.

Steven began to shovel the sand. As it went in, Linda's thin chest shook. She was silent as the tears came from her. She suffered Adie to put her arm about her and seemed to find comfort in it.

Steven spoke the only words, the single benediction. From a choked throat he explained, "I'll make him a mark with his name on it."

The sun, a massive glow of fiery red, lipped above the sea as he moved the last earth upon the grave.

Twenty-One

BACK AT THE HOUSE Steven told Adie, "I don't know, rightly, what to do about the medicine for your ma. There's got to be a man here."

"I can do," said Linda.

There was Adie against his debt to Jesse. There was Linda herself and the two in the other room. "You ain't going to try," he told Linda. "The firewood's all used up. You got to have food."

"We kin use the government stores."

"You need fresh, too, for her," Steven said. "I'll get you fish and clams, some spiny lobster, and cut palmetto cabbage." He looked worriedly at Adie because of being able to offer nothing to her.

"I'll keep on to the Beach," Adie told him.

"I expect you'd be safe enough from here," Steven conceded slowly. "You can send Quimby down. Tomorrow, or even maybe tonight, you can get a schooner to Miami. There's bound to be one there, from waiting out the blow, and it'll be faster than walking back."

"I'll take the mail, too," Adie said.

He looked at her. "I don't want you burdened down."

"Just the bag isn't heavy. It's late now and will be later if I don't take it."

Adie wanted to leave at once, but Steven and Linda wouldn't let her go without having food. Afterward, Steven walked a short way with her.

Never had they seemed so close. The experiences of yesterday and last night, and Adie's lone walk along the beach, made her more a part of the country than ever, and of him.

Now she was carrying the mail for him, holding it on her slim shoulder. Yet it was no time for him to speak of himself with her. Jesse's death was too fresh. Adie herself had her own acute concern.

Adie spoke of something else when they stopped and she was to go on alone. "Steven, they aren't going to take Hypoluxo from you?"

"They got a good start."

"But they can't!" Resolutely, she said, "I'll talk to Sylvanus again."

Steven looked away. He didn't resent as much her appealing to Sylvanus as he did that she still believed the boomer's protestations about being helpless to save the island for him. No matter how convincing the man had been, Steven was incensed with that. "I don't want you asking any favors of him for me."

"Then I'll talk to the others."

"It don't do any good," Steven said flatly.

"But Sylvanus said—"

Steven spoke bitterly. "It does less good with him. I told you how I felt about that."

Adie looked annoyed. "You're being stubborn, Steven."

"Might be I am."

"Just because—"

"I'm telling you, Adie," he said stiffly, "I don't want it brought up with him."

They stared at each other. Steven realized how much the strain of the past few days had made their tempers short. He was aghast that they should be speaking angrily to each other. It was like a sudden storm that had sprung up with no warning, to find them without cover.

He was about to speak in a pacifying tone, but Adie turned and began to walk away.

He wanted to call to her, or run after her, but his pride wouldn't let him. He stood, waiting for her to turn and wave. She kept on going.

Linda told him, "You'll go a sight to find another like her.

She's got gumption. Don't you put yoreself in the way of losin' her."

"You're offering your advice too late," he informed her. "I just got her mad at me."

When Linda heard what it was about, she scoffed, "It don't amount to a little thing."

"Maybe at your age it don't," Steven said gloomily. "Maybe we ain't got that much sense."

"It'll blow over."

"Then I wish the wind would come quick." He was still appalled that he and Adie had fought. He forced himself to change the subject. "I don't reckon Quimby would want the job regular, being a bachelor. You thought any on what you're going to do?"

"There ain't but one thing," the old lady said. "When they git another keeper, we'll move back to the lake."

"You'll be fixed," Steven promised.

"We kin git along by ourselves," Linda declared. "Anybody who starves in this country has got his own self to blame."

"That's all right for a man, not two women and a baby." Steven had already planned other things. "Doc's been complaining of the work at the store since so many new people come. Womenfolk, too, ask for things he don't know about. What reason is there why Della can't work in the store?"

Linda regarded him with a wise look around her wrinkled eyes. "There ain't any," she replied, "iffen he wants her like anybody else. But you got to rid yorself of the notion you're beholden to us on account of what's come about."

He stared at the sky. "One thing I got to do is hunt them combers and give them the same as they give Jesse."

Linda, who had softened since yesterday, reverted to her old self for a moment. "I'll thank you to let me have a part on that."

Quimby arrived the following morning. "I come as quick as I could," he said. "It's easier traveling at night, anyway, with this heat. Adie got a schooner down. I'm pure sorry to hear about Jesse."

Steven saw Della before he went back to Palm Beach. He hadn't dared before. But when Linda told him Della wanted to see him, he went in. With him he carried a fresh bunch of the tiny bananas she liked so much.

At the sight of them now she shook her head and turned her face to the wall. He stood looking at her, and at the child nestling her arm. Her face was pasty. When she turned back to look down at her baby, no smile, but a tender fondness played about her lips.

"I made Jesse a cross," he told her. "I burned his name with a hot poker on the crossboard."

Her eyes were steady when she lifted them to him. In a voice that was not much more than a whisper she said, "Steven, there isn't any cause to regret. It won't do any good. I want a promise from you: you won't go on taking it as you do."

The speech tired her. Only in small part meaning it, but putting conviction in his voice, Steven told her, "I'll try my best."

She searched him with her gaze. Assured, she looked down to her arm. "Do you like him?"

He answered only with the expression on his face. That was enough to bring the ghost of a smile to her lips.

In the afternoon, when he reached the lake, Steven saw that the Margaret D was gone. It had carried the cargo of wine kegs and casks to Jacksonville. Other boats were at the dock, including the white naphtha launch with its stubby smokestack. The launch was off its schedule being tied up at Palm Beach overnight; its home port was Juno. Steven wondered what it meant.

Doc was alone in the store. "Too bad about Jesse," he said. "I couldn't believe it. After Adie told me, I blame myself for not curing you of the drink effects. Except then it might have been you. Them combers," he raged, "has got to—"

He was interrupted by arguing voices. Men began to come into the store. Baker and Durgan were debating with a tall, well-dressed man who had a soft voice and a conciliatory manner.

"He's the representative of the Celestial Railroad," Doc told Steven. "We been holding a political meeting the last two days," he explained. "We ain't been able to decide anything. Another session's to be held right now. You better stay for it, Stevie. The way it'll come out might mean all the difference between you keeping Hypoluxo or not."

The discussion began. A lake man said, "With more people here than any other single place in this end of the county, I can't see why there's been any question at all about having the seat in Palm Beach."

"Maybe you got more people," Baker countered, "but alone you won't win the election to get the site here unless we throw in our votes from the north. Waveland still goes with Jupiter to have it there."

"Palm Beach is where it belongs," Doc stated flatly.

"I am only voicing the wishes of the Jupiter voters," Maple offered. "As I've told you, they will vote for Miami before they'll vote for the lake."

"Jupiter's got nothing like the importance here," Durgan began, when he was drowned out by a man shouting, "Jupiter! We won't hear of nothing else!"

Another man cried, "Get the election first! Then we can decide on where to have the courthouse."

This suggestion found no favor. The argument continued, rising heatedly.

In the midst of it the railroad representative spoke for the first time. "Gentlemen," he said, "it still seems to me that you have two divisions to consider. First the county is divided against itself, and then you, the north end, are divided among yourselves. Unless you can agree, you can achieve nothing. I'm sure you must see now that to settle it is to locate the site right in the middle of your argument, at Juno."

"There ain't anything there," was the objection to this,

"except five families and the narrow-gauge terminus speaking for itself."

"It isn't only the railroad I'm speaking for," the representative pointed out. "It's a compromise for yourselves. And you can put something at Juno—a fine new courthouse."

It was the vision of this that fired them into agreement. Doc finally muttered, "I expect I can get up there easier than down to Miami, with the launch and it being only eight miles."

A vote was called for. Juno, with the exception of Durgan's mischievous "Nay" received every man's agreement.

Steven understood what Doc meant about his keeping or losing Hypoluxo. The State Land Office had written that it had no record of Uncle Charlie's Notice of Final Proof. Doc, pondering this, said, "The more I think of it the more I recall Uncle Charlie saying he'd filled it out. In them days it went to the county clerk at Miami for local recording before being sent on to the Land Office. I got a good idea of what happened. It wasn't sent on, and is still down there, or was until Piggott showed it to Hurley."

Now, in combining the votes of the north end of the county, lay the only chance to win the election and obtain the power and perhaps the record to show that the island belonged to Steven. It was almost like getting or not getting Adie. In his mind she and Hypoluxo were so closely tied that one would not do without the other. And he had made things worse for such a consummation by fighting with Adie.

Twenty-Two

CHARMING TIGER WAS CAMPED on the river bank at Miami. Steven arrived just in time, for the Seminole was starting on another assortment of brandied cherries and whisky. Tiger sat under the shelter previously built for him by his squaws, who crouched at a distance.

"Wy-oh-mey?" Tiger invited, holding up a bottle.

Steven accepted, to humor him. He lifted the bottle to his mouth, but didn't open his lips to let any of the liquor trickle in. He remembered his promise to Jesse.

Tiger nodded, working his chins with satisfaction. He tilted the bottle himself. Steven waited for him to speak, showing him deference.

Tiger waved to the north. "Him take boat," he said. "Wrong man die. Bad."

Steven wondered how he knew. The crew of the schooner who brought Adie to Miami might have spread the news. On the other hand, Tiger could also know more directly. Steven became wary.

The men, he agreed with Tiger, were bad. He pointed out to the Indian that when a man in his tribe was responsible for the death of another, the culprit was tortured to death at the annual Green Corn Dance. Punishment should be given to the beachcombers. It was right and just now that Tiger tell him where they were to be found.

Tiger digested that. For a moment it appeared as though he might divulge the secret. Then he shook his head slowly. "White man thing, not Seminole," he said.

"This man bad, ojus," Steven argued.

"Me good, ojus," Tiger answered. He reiterated his former stand. "I tell him nobody know from me."

Steven knew it was useless to try to persuade him further. Once a Seminole got something in his head there was no taking it out. This was especially true if it was a matter of dealing with his word or his honor. Again, though he had expected to learn of Theron and his men, Steven felt he could trust Tiger. "You let me know other things about them?" he asked.

Tiger pondered, then said, "Something now. Wy-oh-mey?" he invited again.

A second time Steven went through the ritual of pretending to drink with Tiger. He waited while Tiger sucked from the bottle himself.

The Indian said, "Him come here once more—many time. He make friend with trader."

"With other one, too?" Steven inquired. The reference was enough for Tiger to know he meant Sylvanus.

"Him, too."

Steven asked Tiger if Theron and his men had come to Miami after Jesse died at Hillsborough.

"Not after," Tiger replied. "Some time soon before."

Steven wondered if Sylvanus had gone to the length of encouraging the beachcombers to remove the boat. He felt a desire to establish this beyond that to pay back the combers themselves.

"Tiger keep telling you," the Indian promised.

Steven thanked him. Tiger had one more thing to mention. Flourishing his bottle, he said, "You want squaw here—you take her. Other see her much."

The Indian heaved with his silent laughter as Steven left him.

In the trading post Sylvanus looked up at him from where he worked at a table over a plat of Miami showing lots marked off. Bunnell stood with papers in his hand; his concentration on them left him and he said to Steven, "I guess what you people at the lake are trying to do ain't going to work. You can't agree even among yourselves."

"Then you ain't heard the latest," Steven told him.

Both Bunnell and Sylvanus looked at him.

"We agreed," Steven said. "All votes will go for Juno."

Bunnell was indignant. "You can't do that," he threatened. "It ain't right. I don't think it's even legal."

"Like trying to steal Hypoluxo from me?" Steven asked. His question, additionally, was to find out how far they had progressed with the theft. He learned nothing from the trader's reply.

"Now you look here, Pierton," Bunnell stormed. "You keep coming here to say things like that and you won't be welcome any more. You're with the lake, and against us, and—"

"I don't believe we have to worry, Dan," Sylvanus said.

Emily appeared in the doorway at the side of the store. She looked at Steven, at Sylvanus, and then at Steven again. Her eyes expressed a new glee. She said to her brother, "Clara and I are ready to sign the papers if you want." She disappeared.

"Here's the mail," Steven said. He took it from his haversack and put it on the counter.

Bunnell looked irritably at the papers in his hands. "I'm too busy for that now."

"You mind if I take out the Titus letters?" Steven asked.

"I don't care what you do." Bunnell strode out of the store.

Steven guessed Emily and Clara were going in with the Company on the land they owned. He went behind the counter, found the key for the padlock, and opened the mail bag. He selected three letters and put them in his pocket.

He came out from behind the counter and sat on a chair at one end of it near Sylvanus at the table. He began to brush sand from his bare feet. He didn't speak and Sylvanus said nothing.

Sylvanus's silence—unusual and not at all characteristic—made Steven realize for the first time how much of a rival he was in the other man's eyes. Beneath the boomer's pretense of not taking him seriously, he regarded him very seriously indeed. This told Steven one other thing. Sylvanus meant what he once said about Adie. He had lied to himself; he had changed; he not only sounded as if he meant everything he said about Adie, he actually did mean it.

Steven's value as a rival encouraged him. The other fact frightened him. He saw more than ever how, with Sylvanus sincere, Adie could believe him.

He rolled down his trousers. When he spoke it was with care not to quarrel with the man. That way he would find out nothing of what he meant to ask. He inquired, "You heard about Jesse Paget being killed?"

Sylvanus looked up from his plat. "A sad thing," he said. "But 'killing,' Steven? From the men of the schooner I gathered it was an accident."

"That's what it's being called. Anyway, by them who took the boat away." He watched the look on the other man's face closely.

Sylvanus's expression didn't flicker. "Who would do that?"

"I wouldn't know any more than you," Steven said.

Again Sylvanus showed only proper concern. "You mean Theron," he said, "the beachcombers. They thought it would be you to swim the river."

"I didn't say that."

"It follows naturally after what you did to them, doesn't it? I am merely assuming, of course."

Steven pulled on his socks, then one shoe. "I hear the combers been in here a good deal lately."

"They have." Sylvanus gave his easy laugh.

"I hear you made friends with them."

Sylvanus regarded him evenly. "Steven," he said, "if you think anyone actually caused Paget's death, meaning it for you, you ought to take it up with the sheriff."

"I never liked talking to thin air." Steven put on the other shoe and stood up. He was sure he had what he wanted. Sylvanus had been just a little too casual, a bit too prepared. But Steven realized that he was too slippery ever to be caught through himself.

"You're going to see Adie?" Sylvanus inquired.

"Might be."

"Good luck." He seemed wise in something.

Steven stared at him, and told him, "For some uses, I wish I could lie like you."

Again Sylvanus laughed.

The rutted sand path leading through the palm woods to the Titus homestead had been somewhat cleared. At one side of it, before the house was reached, Steven heard the sound of chopping. Titus was working in the scrub, hacking at it with an ax, and piling what he cut to be burned. He was in his shirtsleeves, which were stained with perspiration. He saw Steven, who stopped and went over to him.

Titus looked at him with slight hesitancy. But he said nothing about what brought this to his manner. He told Steven, "I'm clearing the land. Sylvanus Hurley thinks it will sell better this way."

"You get yourself a machete to use," Steven suggested, "and it'll go easier."

Titus wiped his forehead with an arm. "I have realized that," he said, "and mean to do it." Gazing at his work, he went on, "I'm not sure I am doing the right thing in the first place. I don't like that Company much. I went in with it only because everyone else has and I didn't want to be left behind."

Steven murmured, "I couldn't tell you about that."

Titus glanced toward his house. He sounded regretful when he said, "I can't ask you to visit with Adela, Steven. Her mother has been low, very low, and she must be with her almost every minute of the time. I'm sorry, my boy."

"That's all right," Steven told him.

Titus, Steven thought, was uncomfortable. It might have come from advising him against going on to the house and this lack of hospitality. It might come from another thing. Steven determined to find out.

"It ain't anything else?" he asked. "Anything about Adie and me?"

Titus wiped his face before he replied. "Why—well, she

did say something about being put out with you. She did not explain what it was. And I can't for the life of me imagine. Certainly it is of no consequence."

Steven tried to decide if Titus's explanation sounded lame, or if that was only in his imagination. It was enough, in any case, to strike him with dread.

He nursed the dread, against his will, after he gave Titus the letters and went back to the trading post. He remembered how wise Sylvanus had been. And according to Tiger, Sylvanus was seeing Adie. Of course he might, being here all the week, be doing this at moments when it was possible for her to leave her mother. Then again it could be more significant than that. Steven wondered if warning had been given him not to go near Adie.

Twenty-Three

DOC TOLD THE STORY of Hypoluxo with every purchase. Cap Jim spread it up and down the coast. Doc urged Steven to spend some time electioneering. A great deal depended on how many registered to vote, and people needed prodding about this. Dewey Durgan, who had been appointed Supervisor of Elections for the north end of the county, with a wave of his hand made Steven his assistant. Steven asked:

"Is there anything against taking the registration books to folks at their houses? That'll save them one trip, they only having to come in once then to vote."

"Ain't any reason I can see," Doc opined. He asked Durgan, "What do you think, Supervisor?"

"If there was a reason," Durgan replied, "I hereby revoke it."

Steven took a week off from his mail-walking duties. He hired Quimby, who came up from staying with the Pagets after putting in extra supplies for them, to make the trip. The first three days Steven spent in visiting people who lived up and down the lake and inland, those who infrequently came in to the store. Traveling by boat and on foot, he found the prospective voters almost as interested in his personal problems as they were in getting the county seat located at Juno. One man said, "I'll help anybody get the woman he wants."

Steven didn't quite know how he reached this conclusion.

"Great snakes alive," the man said, "if Miami wins, that Hurley down there will control everything. He'll be the best catch in the county and he'll get what he wants, including your girl."

The election issues more clarified in his mind than ever, Steven redoubled his efforts. He boarded the naphtha launch on its afternoon trip, carrying the registration books with him. Doc cautioned, "Don't forget to tell everybody to vote for me for county clerk. And Baker for sheriff—if we got to have the law officer in this end, we want somebody with backbone."

The launch began to puff. Horrible fumes came from its funnel. It left the dock and started up the lake. Steven was the only passenger. He sat up forward on a bench, out of the waft of the naphtha fumes, and near the serious young man who ran the boat. "You registered for the election yet?" Steven asked him.

"I'll do it later." The man, a newcomer brought down from the North to operate the launch, was more concerned with his chugging engine than he was in the election.

Steven opened the Jupiter book. "Sign here right now."

He was disappointed in Juno. A tiny railroad station stood a short way back from the shore at the head of the lake. There was a dock for the launch, a warehouse at the foot of the dock, and five unpainted frame houses.

The train stood in front of the station. It consisted of a

wheezy little wood-burning engine, a passenger coach, and a boxcar. It had come from Jupiter with the engine at the head of the train, and with no means of getting itself about, it had to run backward on the return journey.

Steven knew Captain Matheson, the conductor. For years before he turned to railroading, the genial old man was a fisherman, and Steven had often accompanied him. They hailed each other, and Steven asked if there would be time for him to register the people in the houses before the train left.

"Time?" asked the Captain. He tipped back his yacht cap, as faded as Steven's. He seemed puzzled. "Why, you go right ahead, Stevie, and let me know when you're ready to leave."

Steven obtained the names he wanted, and the promise of the people to go in to Jupiter on election day and vote. Then Captain Matheson boosted him aboard the coach, and climbed on himself. The Captain jerked the signal cord running overhead along the length of the narrow little car. With a jerk, the train started, the engine snorting and issuing billows of acrid black smoke from its tall stack.

Again Steven was the only passenger. Captain Matheson, sitting beside him on one of the seats, said, "Lots more going down than the other way. The country is opening up, Stevie, yes, sir, it surely is going ahead. Faster than we can go backward."

Steven, looking out the window, his body rocking to the violent sway of the coach on the narrow-gauge track, felt he was on a toy train. Suddenly it came to a stop. On either side there was nothing except woods. Then he saw a small shack near the track. There was no sign of it being inhabited. "What's this?" he asked.

"This," announced the Captain, "is the city of Venus. One of our important stops, though nobody ever gets on." He reached up and pulled the signal cord and the train began to back up again. "Nobody ever gets on at the way stations," he continued. "You watch."

The Captain's word was good. After another mile had been

covered, the train once again screeched to a stop. Looking out, Steven saw that it had passed a family consisting of a man, his wife, and child, who now walked down the track toward the train, which reversed itself to go to meet them. When they came aboard, Steven asked the man to register. He obeyed, saying surprisingly, "You're the fellow we've got to vote for to keep his island, ain't you?"

On its eight-mile journey the Celestial Railroad prudently took shelter behind the beach ridge. Only here and there did there come a glimpse of the ocean. When Steven saw the beach he compared his walking pace with the speed of the train. It would take him the better part of three hours to cover the distance on the giving sand. The train, if it ran steadily, could do it in half an hour.

He understood then that it wouldn't be many years before a regular railroad ran along here, all the way to Miami, just as Doc had predicted. Walking the beach would become a thing of the past. It gave him a queer feeling of life changing, turning over, and of good, familiar things passing.

The train stopped at the city of Mars, a duplicate of Venus. It stopped again when it ran out of fuel and the engineer and the Negro fireman spent twenty minutes loading a supply of fatwood from a prepared pile along the right of way. The last stop before reaching Jupiter was made when a man hailed it from the woods, to shout to Captain Matheson above the puffing of the engine:

"Here's that venison I promised you!" A whole hind quarter was flung up on the vestibule.

"Wait a minute," Steven said. He got out with his book and held it for the man, saying, "Sign here."

Jupiter was encouraging for the size of the vote that might be turned out. When Steven had last been here only three cabbage houses stood near the foot of the towering red-brick lighthouse. Now there were nearly two dozen frame dwellings. It was a town, clustered about the light, with its own store, and a big white shallow-draft steamer at a long new dock in

Hobe Sound. Most miraculously of all, a telegraph wire ran north on low poles, connecting Jupiter with the rest of the nation.

Doc was jubilant over Steven's report when he returned. "We're going to win," he declared, "without a question of a doubt. I wouldn't be surprised if we had a hundred voting."

Steven didn't know where they were coming from. A few over a hundred had registered in the section between Waveland and the lake. But rarely did all the registrants, or anything like their number, actually come in to vote. A good deal depended on the election-day weather; if it was bad, many wouldn't bother to make an often difficult trip.

Following Steven's next trip to Miami, Doc changed his tune and admitted that there was some doubt about the results. Steven could obtain no definite information about Miami's political moves. Bunnell and the others would tell him nothing. They were keeping secret any estimate of their vote. Because of many new settlers, Miami's election figures of past years could not be counted on any more than those of the lake region. Each end of the county was baffled by the other.

Steven didn't see Adie in Miami. Her father came for the mail. Titus restricted himself to saying that his wife was no better. Steven looked at him, and at Sylvanus, for any sign that Adie had made a fearful decision. He saw none. The Bunnell sisters reversed their attitude toward him. Their behavior had always been strange, and now, when they told Steven it would be a good thing for the world if he could best Sylvanus, their about-face was disquieting instead of being reassuring.

In the middle of October the weather broke the day Cap Jim and Gerald sailed with the new keeper and his family for the house of refuge, bringing back the Pagets. At last the long monotony of the summer heat and rains came to an end. For three days the wind blew out of the northeast, the first time it had come from that direction for seven months. To Steven its paramount importance was its effect on the health of Mrs. Titus. If it was enough to make her mother well again, Adie could think of other things. She could think of him—or of Sylvanus.

Twenty-Four

ON ELECTION DAY the northeast wind blew again. This time it set up a gale, thrashing the trees and stirring the lake roughly. It was far from inviting for people to sail or row to the store to cast their votes. The dark stormy day was a better one to stay home indoors.

It made Steven nervous and Doc irritable. Dewey Durgan, sitting at a table in the store on which the wooden ballot box was set, did little business. Throughout the morning only a trickle of people came to write their names on ballots and insert them through the slit in the top of the box.

In the afternoon, up until four o'clock, only two voters arrived. Durgan became as gloomy as he always looked but rarely acted. "We might as well give up," he said. "There's only about two hours till sundown when the polls close. I'll take my bottle of Pratt's Gin now instead of waiting."

"You won't do anything of the sort," Doc scolded. "I figure folks is holding off until late so they can stay to get the results of our turn-out."

It was nearly another hour before Doc's estimation began to bear fruit. Across the lake the boats began to appear in twos and threes. Men arrived on foot. A few of them brought their families. They had waited until after their day's work, or until they had an early supper in their stomachs. They meant to remain in the store while the returns came in from farther north in the county.

The lateness of the voting created a problem. There were more people in line than Durgan and Steven could handle before sundown. The voters themselves took up the discussion about whether votes could be cast after the allotted time. Durgan settled it officially by stating, "You can't tell when it's sundown with this sky. Anybody in line at dark can cast his vote if it takes up to midnight."

It took until well after seven, and then the better part of another hour to make the tabulation. Practically every name in the registration book had been checked to note that the man to whom it belonged had appeared.

Steven caught the full excitement of the election when he helped Durgan count the ballots. The store was jam-packed with chattering people as they added and figured, with Doc hanging over the table. Finally Durgan said, "I make it fifty-three for the county seat being at Juno, none against. Doc, you get them all for clerk, and Baker all for sheriff."

Doc announced the result to the crowd, which buzzed with comment and then quieted down to hear the other results. With a red, long face, Durgan admitted thirty-two votes had been cast for temperance and only eleven against; the rest of the voters had refrained from committing themselves on this subject. In defiance, Durgan strode to Doc's medicine shelf, pulled the cork from a bottle of Pratt's Gin and took a long drink. The Deacon made sounds of protest mingled with those of pleasure over the election figures.

The crowd waited restively for the rest of the program. The arrangements for this were of as much interest as the election itself. The Waveland returns were to be sent to Jupiter by telegraph. The Celestial Railroad would make a special run of its locomotive alone to carry the combined Waveland and Jupiter returns to Juno. From there the naphtha launch was to bring them to Palm Beach.

There were many speculations about this plan. It was said

that something would be sure to break down. Most were of the opinion that the launch would never make it at night, but would ground itself somewhere on the lake. Steven, with others, went out to listen for the sound of the launch's coming, returning each time without hearing it.

At ten o'clock it hadn't arrived. Some of the voters went home in disgust.

Finally the puff of the launch was heard as it neared the dock. No one had been outside to see or hear it coming. Steven rushed down to the dock. The operator called out the figures to him before he handed over the papers on which they were written. To Steven there was only one of real importance. The upcountry vote for the courthouse was fifty-three, exactly the same as that of Palm Beach.

In the store Doc announced triumphantly, "That's a hundred and six!" A look of exultation came over his face. Then he sobered.

The evenly divided vote caused a good deal of amusement that the compromise on Juno had come out so fairly. Durgan, waving his arms recklessly, cheered, "Miami'll never touch it!"

Doc shook his head. "Maybe it will. You can't tell what that crowd down there will do."

Dewey Durgan hadn't been sober enough to sign the official report on his election district's returns. That could come later. Steven carried the figures in his head. The news rode with him lightly along the beach, and with it went an expectation.

No matter what the result of the election, Steven had decided to have it out with Adie. It was past time for wild speculation on how she felt, past time for worry about their spat, long past time for inability to speak. He meant to know.

He would see her, without care of how her mother was. She could spare him that important moment. Finally he would declare himself and have her answer. She would take Sylvanus or she would take him.

In his eagerness to reach her he arrived at Miami several

hours before his usual time. Only a handful of people saw him coming and gathered in front of the store to await his walk up the dock. There were Bunnell and his sisters, Sylvanus, the sheriff, and Piggott. They were trying to show they weren't worried by not coming to meet him.

As he strode toward the trading post Steven caught a glimpse of a man ducking back around the corner of the building. He had the impression that there was something wrong with the man's left arm, that it flapped at his side.

Almost certainly it was Theron.

For an instant he wanted to let the election returns, Adie, and the mail go in favor of searching out the beachcomber. Then he decided to take that up later, waiting until there were fewer people around. It would be a matter between him and Theron alone, with interference from no one else.

Sylvanus was the first to accost him. Cheerily he asked, while the others hung on the question, "What's your vote, Steven?"

Steven didn't answer. He was still thinking about Theron. He strode on into the store, followed by all of them. He delivered the mail. He tried not to fear that Miami had received more votes than Juno.

"What's this hocus-pocus?" Bunnell demanded. "Come on, give us your figures."

Steven regarded the trader evenly. In back of him were Emily and Clara. Their eyes were bright with friendliness and expectation. Their curious behavior disturbed him, but not enough for him to fail to remember Doc's instructions. "What's yours?" he asked Bunnell.

"We asked first," the trader retorted.

Sylvanus's laugh came. "Don't you trust us, Steven?"

Piggott, with courage drawn from those about him, said, "We ain't got anything to hide here. But you're acting like you had something."

"You tell me yours first," Steven directed Bunnell.

"I won't do it," the trader stated. "I won't do anything of the kind."

"I know what he's doing," Oat McCarty reasoned belatedly. "After we say we got more votes than him, he'll change his to a bigger figure."

Steven replied, "That works both ways."

There were glares. Steven didn't try to return them, but simply held his ground. When he looked at Sylvanus he saw in his eyes an amused respect.

"I suggest," Sylvanus told him, "you write on a slip of paper what you have to say. And Dan," he instructed Bunnell, "you write the Miami figures on another slip. Then both of you pass them over to each other at the same time."

With this Steven was satisfied. Bunnell, grumbling, agreed.

There was deep silence in the trading post as the slips of paper changed hands. Steven, devouring quickly what had been written on the one he received, saw that opposite the name Miami had been noted "80" and that "2" was put after Juno. They hadn't attempted to pad the vote, thinking their eighty would be more than enough.

He had won. He would keep the island.

He kept his eyes down, glancing at the other figures on the paper. He looked up as Bunnell howled.

"It ain't possible!" the trader choked.

Steven was more interested in how Sylvanus received it. He had taken the slip of paper from Bunnell and now, while the sheriff and Piggott crowded around to look, he was regarding it with genuine surprise. A faint frown showed on his face, the first Steven had ever seen there.

While Emily and Clara were heard to giggle and their brother caught his breath, Steven addressed Sylvanus, "I see you got two with enough sense to vote the right way."

The effort Sylvanus had to put forth to keep his feelings from his voice was evident when he said, "The Misses Bunnell, who appear to have some queer feelings and be on your side, talked two voters into going back on their own interests."

Emily and Clara, ruffled at being the focus of attention,

flounced out. They smiled strangely at Steven as they passed him.

Bunnell found his voice again. "Now you look here, Pierton!" he stormed. "You know as good as we do you ain't got that many people up there!"

"You mean," Steven replied, "you know it now as good as you did before."

"No matter how you put it," Bunnell spluttered, "you and Bethune and them others ain't going to put over on us anything like that."

"There ain't any question of putting over on you," Steven said. "It's voted. And we put everybody else in office all down the line, including temperance and the sheriff."

Oat McCarty glowered.

Bunnell had been looking at Sylvanus. "Well," he now said, "we ain't going to accept it. You couldn't have done anything else but stuff the boxes. It ain't a proper election, and we're protesting it."

Piggott whispered in the trader's ear. Bunnell then stated, "And you ain't got the legal statement on it. You ain't brought anything except what you say."

"I'll have that next trip," Steven said. "And there wasn't any stuffing. You can't—"

"It's no good at all," Bunnell announced. "We'll fight the election to the last ditch. We ain't giving up the seat and that's the beginning and end of it."

"You got to give it up," Steven stated.

Again Bunnell consulted Sylvanus with his glance, and as if encouraged, replied, "How you going to make us? We got the county records. As long as they're here, we keep the seat. You can't run the county without the records."

"You'll be made to give them up," Steven said.

"How you going to do it?" Bunnell demanded. "We'll keep investigating the election till you wished you never heard of it. We'll bring up things like you taking the registration books around with you—we know about that and it ain't regular. And all the time don't forget we keep the seat. What's more," he went on, "I don't think we want you coming here until your end of the county gets over its ideas it won. We can't have you bringing any ideas like that."

"You mean," Steven accused slowly, "you don't want me to bring the official paper showing we won."

"You can take it any way you like," the trader said. "From now on, nobody from up there is welcome here."

Steven considered. "You're going too far saying that. I come here for the government with the mail."

"You don't have to worry about our mail. We'll get along through Key West and when a schooner comes."

Steven told him, "I mean to keep bringing it just the same."

"You do," threatened Bunnell, "and you see what kind of a reception you get."

"There's other things I come here for, too," Steven said hotly. "You won't keep me away from them."

They all knew what he meant.

Jocularly, Sylvanus said, "Maybe you'd be interested to know that Mrs. Titus has recovered almost completely. She's well enough so that Adie doesn't have to stay with her now. She can think of—let's say, her own life."

A third time, while Piggott and Oat listened with intense interest, Bunnell consulted Sylvanus with his look. Each time he seemed to ask if he had gone too far. And now, when Sylvanus nodded, he received permission to go further.

"In fact," Bunnell informed Steven, "we don't want you staying here a minute more right now."

Steven said tightly, looking at Sylvanus. "You mean he don't. Maybe he can put you through other tricks, but he won't—"

"I'm declaring you," Bunnell said, "a public nuisance here in Miami. And I'm asking the sheriff to put you out."

Oat shuffled his feet. He came forward a little, eying Steven. He looked mean. "You heard what Mister Bunnell said."

"You ain't the sheriff any more," Steven told him, "and you never been enough sheriff to lay a finger on me."

Oat's eyes shifted, and when they came back again, they were meaner than ever. "I'm enough sheriff to put an arrest on you. If you act up a fuss there's others who'll help me to put you in jail."

Steven thought of Theron. The other two beachcombers must be here, too. Added to them would be Sylvanus and Bunnell. He looked about, hoping to see Adie come in the door. He raged, "You ain't got a jail here that can hold me."

The sheriff said, "You can be shot for escaping."

Sylvanus said, as if he had nothing to do with it and merely offered sensible advice, "I'd go if I were you."

"You got plenty of time to row across the bay while it's still light," Bunnell pointed out, "if you don't waste any. And don't try to sneak back tonight. We'll be watching, with a bullet for you."

For a moment more Steven regarded them. He saw that Oat would carry out his threat. The man hated him because of the low estimation in which he held him, and because of his part in getting him elected out of office.

Without questioning the trader about the upgoing mail, Steven picked up his haversack and went out of the store. Oat and Bunnell followed him, with Sylvanus and Piggott close behind. They waited while he walked down the dock to his rowboat.

Steven made his way as slowly as he could. He kept watching for Adie. He wished he could call through the trees to her, that her house was not so far away. He considered rowing up the river to her instead of starting across the bay. He decided against it when he remembered the look in Oat's eyes.

As he got in his boat he heard a splashing sound coming from up the river. He turned, to see Charming Tiger sitting in the middle of a dugout canoe. His wives, one at each end, paddled.

They couldn't stop him from speaking to Tiger. He called to the Indian, and the Seminole waved back and spoke to his wives to paddle toward Steven.

The two craft touched, and Tiger said, "His-see."

Steven repeated the greeting, calling Tiger, "Friend." Then he waved upriver in the direction of the Titus homestead and asked, "You tell squaw message for me?"

"Tell," agreed Tiger.

A shout came from the trading post. Oat started toward the dock. Steven thought rapidly to choose words that would be intelligible to the Indian as well as to Adie. "Say to her," he instructed Tiger, "Wait, I see her."

The Seminole pointed to Steven and repeated, "Wait, I see her."

Steven pushed off as another shout came. The rowboat and dugout separated. He pleaded to Tiger, "Tell her now, before wy-oh-mey."

Tiger nodded. He was puzzled by Steven's actions and the calls from the trading post.

Steven rowed away, across the bay, wondering if Tiger would remember correctly or if he would remember at all.

Twenty-Five

INDIGNATION RAN HIGH among the group of lake citizens gathered outside the store. "It's just like Dan Bunnell," Doc stormed, "to do a thing like that."

"It ain't him so much," Steven claimed. "He ain't so bad

left alone by himself. It's Sylvanus leading him, ever since the boomer went to Miami, that's what's doing it."

"No matter who's doing it," Cap Jim growled, "we can't let Miami try such a thing on us."

Some were for taking it up with higher authorities at once. Writing to the governor was suggested, even to Washington City.

Doc pointed out, "The more we get tangled up in that kind of thing the worse it'd be. And look what would be happening all the while—Miami keeping the seat. To say nothing of Steven not keeping his island. They'll grab it from him while we're fussing with the law."

"I don't see how but there's only one thing to do," Dewey Durgan proposed. "And I don't see why we don't do it."

"I was thinking all along the beach," Steven agreed, "that it would be easy."

"You mean take the records by force?" the Deacon asked. "Steal them?"

"You call it stealing?" Doc asked. "When we won them fair and square? They're the ones doing the stealing."

Cap Jim was ahead of them all. He glanced at the afternoon sky. "There wouldn't be time to get there in the Margaret D for tonight with this whiff of wind blowing. Tomorrow night's the time, and the only thing against us will be a moon, full out if there ain't clouds."

Gerald, standing at his side, looked expectant. He rubbed his hands together as if he itched to be under way.

They were arranging the party and making tentative plans when a Seminole dugout was sighted coming up the lake. Steven recognized the bulk of Charming Tiger paddling it. Anxiously, he went down to the shore to meet it.

While he waited he wondered again at the Indian way through the Glades that permitted Tiger to get here by canoe not long after he covered the same distance on foot along the beach.

Tiger grounded his dugout, set his turban aright, fingered his watch chain and safety pins, and clambered out. To Steven's question about delivering his message to Adie, Tiger nodded soberly.

"What did she say?" Steven wanted to know.

Tiger looked away, indicating that he had bad news to impart. "She take other to marry," he said.

Steven didn't think Tiger knew what he was saying. "You've got it wrong," he told the Indian.

Tiger shook his head. He meant exactly what he said. Steven insisted that he couldn't have told Adie what he instructed him to say. Tiger repeated the message, and then repeated the one he had brought. "Too late," he told Steven, looking at him with his black bold eyes.

When the fat Indian broke into his silent laughter, Steven resented it for the first time.

He barely heard the other news Tiger brought and imparted to the group in front of the store. The Miami people suspected that an attempt might be made to steal the records. Theron and his two men had been delegated to guard them. The cunning of this was seen at once. By having the beachcombers do the work, the onus of illegally keeping the records would be at least partially removed from anyone else in case there was real trouble.

Gerald gave expression to the best feeling about this. "If we got up the intention for true," the little Conch said, "wot makes it more better?" He seemed worried that the trip to obtain the records might not now be carried out.

Cap Jim boomed at him with approval, "Everybody be ready earlier than I said first, to be certain sure we get down there in time."

"We'll show them combers a thing or two," Doc stormed, "and it's past time somebody did."

A number of men, including Quimby, clamored to go along, but Cap Jim held the group down to himself, Doc, Steven, Gerald, and Durgan. As an election official, Durgan would lend their own aspect of legality to the proceedings. Charming Tiger agreed to accompany them on the sharpie; he might be very useful. Cap Jim told the others that it wasn't force needed, but trickery to meet trickery.

Steven could barely wait for morning to come. He lay sleepless, thinking about Adie. The records, even Hypoluxo, were small parts of the events ahead. He couldn't believe it yet. He had questioned Tiger still again, to ascertain beyond any doubt that the Indian understood everything.

During the past weeks he had speculated on how much Adie might be missing him, if it could be any portion of the amount he yearned for her. He was certain that she thought of him. But now it seemed that if she did, it wasn't enough. Surely she knew, even if he hadn't said it in so many words, that he wanted her, that it was his life to have her. It must be mistakenly, then, that he had counted on the same from her, thinking he saw this in her as well.

One part of him grasped with cold dread the announcement that she had accepted Sylvanus. Another part refused to credit it. He called out to her not to do it. He told her all the things about Sylvanus he hadn't told her because she would think he spoke only out of jealousy. He warned her, crying that he wouldn't let her do it if only for her own sake.

About one thing he was certain. He would hear from her own lips her decision and make her listen to his plea. He would force his words on her, whether or not she wanted to hear them.

He was haggard in the morning, and impatient for the Margaret D to get under way. The others had gone ahead to the boat and he waited with Doc for Della to come to the store. When she appeared she brought the baby with her in a basket.

"What you doing with him?" Doc asked. "I don't mind you having him here, but—"

"Linda's going with you," Della told him. "That's why I can't leave him with her."

"What kind of an idea has she got?" Doc asked.

Steven and Della, looking at each other, understood together. "Steven will tell you," she said to Doc. "And if I'm hearing right, they're learning at the boat now."

From the dock there came loud voices. Steven and Doc left the store and went down to the boat. On board, sitting on the low rail, were Durgan and Charming Tiger. Camped on the cabin housing was Linda. She was shouting to Cap Jim on the dock, while Gerald stood near her on the deck.

"Come off my boat!" Cap Jim ordered.

"I'm goin'!" Linda called back. "You're after them combers an' that Hurley. They did to Jesse, an' I mean to be along to see you treat them proper."

"We're after the records, no more—unless we got to," Cap Jim told her. "I won't have any interfering old woman aboard my boat!"

"You're goin' to have me!" Linda shrilled.

Raging, Cap Jim motioned to Gerald to put her off.

Gingerly, Gerald laid one hand on Linda's arm. She shook it off, crying, "Don't you tech me, you furriner!"

Cap Jim drew himself up. His beard seemed to explode with sound when he roared, "If you ain't off there before I can get on, I'll put you off myself if I have to do it overside!"

"You won't do no sich thing," Linda informed him, "an' you got the knowin' of it."

Cap Jim didn't carry out his threat. While Durgan and Tiger were amused, he stood helplessly in his tracks.

Doc advised, "Let her come if she wants to that bad."

Outraged, and keeping up a continual oathful muttering, Cap Jim began to cast off. Doc went aboard and Steven, following him, was told by Linda, "Somebody's got to see you attend to the right thing, an' you won't do it with yore worryin' only about Adie. Look here, boy, she ain't goin' to take him. She's got more sense."

Steven wasn't heartened. He helped to push the sharpie away from the dock, and gave Gerald a hand with raising the sails.

It was Doc who caused the next disturbance. Suddenly he cried, "I clean forgot that pistol I borrowed to take along! Put back so I can get—"

Cap Jim turned his glare from Linda to his brother. Standing at the tiller, he growled, "I won't put back for any pistol, you hear me?" He subsided a little and then said, "If there's that kind of work, we can use my rifle aboard."

There was barely enough breeze on the lake to move them. Slowly the Margaret D sailed up to the inlet. Here it was a question of the boat working her way out to the ocean without the southeast wind driving her ashore. Maneuvering carefully, Cap Jim used the outgoing tide more than the breeze. The centerboard scraped the bar, grinding on the bottom. It could be heard rasping up into its slot, and then they floated free.

There was little more wind outside than on the lake. With a full breeze they could head straight down the coast. As it was, they had to tack out nearly to the Stream and then reach in again. Instead of bowling along, they covered distance tortuously, stitching a zigzag through the day.

The light sharpie lifted and responded to every whim of the gentle swell. It made Doc, Tiger, and Durgan seasick. The two white men retired to the cabin. The Indian sat on the floor of the cockpit, the copper cast of his skin tinged with green. Cap Jim nursed his anger for Linda, who lapsed into a stubborn silence as she more fully realized that the beachcombers and Hurley were to be avoided rather than sought out. Steven was glum. Gerald's sardonic skepticism passed for the only good humor aboard.

The inauspicious nature of their start lasted during the entire trip down. It was not improved when the moon, shortly after dark, lifted itself out of the sea into a cloudless sky. The immense orange disk was a threat which soon lighted the world with unbelievable white brilliance. The lines on a hand could be seen in its glare.

The running lights were put out long before they reached the passage way into Biscayne Bay at midnight. The time of their arrival was the only good thing about the voyage so far. The wind, instead of increasing, had dropped to a point where there wasn't enough for the Margaret D's sails to creak her limber masts.

Cap Jim slid the boat into the bay as far as he dared. Gerald eased the anchor silently into the water. They were a quarter of a mile from the freshwater well. "If I go in any more, we won't be able to get out at all on this wind," Cap Jim growled.

The sails were left standing. They gave more chance for the boat to be seen from the shore, but it would be better to have them in readiness. No light showed from Miami.

The sharpie's small boat was put over the side. Cap Jim's ordering of the shore party left Doc and Linda on board. There was, in any case, room only with crowding for five in the small boat. This time Cap Jim stopped Linda by simply standing in her way. "Now you look here," he told her, "it's going to be bad enough with Steve going to that girl of his besides getting the records."

"I don't see what I come for," Linda complained.

"You ain't telling me anything I don't know already," he retorted.

When they had all dropped over the side the several feet down into the small boat, the water was inches from its gunwale. Steven and Gerald rowed with oars working between cloth-wrapped pins. They made no noise as they rowed past the freshwater well and then on toward shore.

They landed on the bay side of the north point of the river. From here they couldn't be seen from the trading post or any of the houses. The boat was pulled up and then they started through the grove of palms to Fort Dallas.

They made their way carefully, keeping in the shadows as much as possible. It was hardly necessary for Tiger to lead them over ground on which they would crackle no stick underfoot, for the moonlight revealed everything with unwelcome clarity.

Fort Dallas loomed through the trees, thirty yards away,

and here they stopped. The building was in darkness. The east side, which they faced, lost itself in shadow. The darkness extended for some feet in front of the building. They stood, watching and examining it. An owl hooted, then hooted again.

Dewey Durgan was of the whispered opinion that no one was here. If that was so, it meant the records had been taken to another place.

"Man," Tiger confided.

Steven, with the others, looked harder. At first he could see nothing. Then he could make out a darker splotch than the gray the walls of the old barracks offered. Someone sat there.

Gerald gave a low hiss. He saw it, too. Almost at the same time his sound came, the splotch moved. The man got up, and emerged into the moonlight. Steven now saw that it wasn't Theron, but the smallest of the beachcombers. Slung in his arm the barrel of a shotgun glittered. He was armed to repel an attack or to fire a signal.

In low tones they debated their procedure. Cap Jim inquired of Tiger if the Indian could get to the man and silence him without an alarm being given. Before Tiger could answer, Steven, who had been studying the ground across the distance to the building, whispered, "I'm going." But even as he spoke, Gerald gave another hiss and was on his way.

Cap Jim swore under his breath. He couldn't call the Conch back for fear of being heard by the comber. Then he told Tiger and Steven, "Maybe he can do it better than both of you."

They watched Gerald disappear to the right among the palms. For a long time they couldn't follow or see him. Finally he emerged some distance away from the end of the building. For a fleeting instant he was a dim silent figure darting through the moonlight. Then he was gone again.

They held their breaths while they watched the corner of the barracks. The comber walked toward it, didn't go all the way to the end, and retraced his steps. As soon as his back was turned, Gerald appeared once more. Like a cat he stole up on the comber. His hands reached like lightning. There was a single, strangling squawk as the man was bent backward. The shotgun slipped out of his arm and dropped to the ground.

Gerald had him flat on his back, industriously choking him when they came up. "Don't go killing him," Cap Jim said, "no matter if he should be."

Gerald was disappointed. He apologized for the noise he had allowed the man. "It were," he said, "on account of me 'aving no practice for too long."

Cap Jim, Tiger, and Durgan began to work on the heavy shutters over the window of the room used for the county commissioners' meetings. The shutters started to give, but the process was long in favor of making no racket. Steven bent to the comber on whose chest Gerald sat. The man's eyes bulged with the Conch's attentions and with fright.

"You going to tell me what Hurley had to do with your taking the boats across the inlets," Steven asked him, "or you want me to turn him loose on you again?" He indicated Gerald.

The man gasped, "Not me—I didn't have nothing—"

Steven gestured to Gerald.

This time the man choked, "Theron planned to do it anyways. But Hurley paid him."

The shutters gave way and were eased open. There being no sash or panes, Cap Jim and Durgan climbed in, with Tiger heaving his bulk after them. Gerald scrambled off the beach-comber and Steven yanked the man to his feet. He ordered him through the window and he and Gerald pulled themselves in.

It was nearly black in the room. Cap Jim risked scratching a match to orient themselves and find the cabinet containing the records. The sulphur fumes rose from the match, making Durgan cough. In the darkness the flimsy door of the cabinet was forced open and Cap Jim began to pass out the ledgers, packets of papers, and seals.

Steven told the beachcomber to get down on the floor. He held him while Gerald stripped the man's belt from him and trussed his hands to his feet, bent up behind him. The man made no sound or protest.

Cap Jim felt in the cabinet to see if he had removed everything. They began to take the records through the window. It wasn't long before they were outside again. Durgan closed the shutters, saying of the beachcomber inside, "Even if he hollers, nobody will hear him from in there."

Now Steven was ready to leave with Tiger on the part of the expedition really important to him. Cap Jim, with his arms full of record books, asked, "You sure you don't want us to wait on the shore?"

"You go ahead with the records," Steven said. "There's no use chancing them. Tiger will get me to the sharpie in a dug-out."

"You know I been against this from the first," Cap Jim growled. "We got what we come for. You can see her another time."

"If anything happens," Steven told him, "and you got to leave me here, I don't want you holding up for a minute."

"Now Steve, you know I couldn't—"

Flatly, Steven said, "You agreed like that."

"You promise not to go near Hurley or that Theron?"

"I agreed like that," Steven said. "You keep to yours and I'll keep to mine."

Cap Jim, Durgan, and Gerald made their way back through the palms. Steven and Tiger headed for the river.

Twenty-Six

FROM THE RIVER SHORE, opposite the trading post, the coals of several Seminole fires glowed dully across the water. Steven knew that Tiger's people, encamped on the bank, were to be feared most. Their curiosity might be aroused by movement at night, making them call out.

Fortunately they didn't have to approach them. They had thought they would have to cross the river by using the ferry and get a dugout there. On the bank, almost at their feet, lay the long slim shape of a canoe.

They launched it and climbed in. Tiger took the paddle at the stern. They dipped into the water without sound, propelling the unwieldy craft slowly upstream, keeping close to the bank. When they came opposite the Titus homestead, they paddled swiftly across. The dugout grounded, and Steven got out. He pulled its prow up on the shore with the Indian still sitting in it.

"Tiger stay here," Steven told the Seminole. He pointed at him and then at himself. "Maybe have to leave quick."

Tiger grunted.

Steven walked to the house. The land was cleared to the river. He passed Titus's coontie mill, plain in the moonlight. He went around to the front of the house. He knew Adie slept here.

Mounting the steps, he was surprised to know how cool he was. Ever since yesterday he had been convinced that nothing could be worse than he expected, that anything else would be better, and now the conviction continued.

He rapped on the door. No sound came from inside. He rapped again, a little harder. Then Adie's sleepy voice was heard. "Who's there?"

"It's me," Steven told her.

It was only after an instant that her voice came from directly behind the door. "Steven!"

"I got to see you."

"Wait," she said through the door.

"Don't light a lamp," he cautioned her. "Tell your folks the same if they get up."

It was some time before he heard her again. While he waited he listened for any sound from the direction of the trading post. There was none. He meant, after he saw Adie, and despite what he told Cap Jim, to pay a visit there. He could treat Theron, and perhaps Sylvanus as well, and then get back to Tiger.

The door opened. Adie had dressed, though her hair hung down about the side of her face. It glinted in the light of the moon coming through the window as she stepped back into the room. Steven went in, closing the door after him.

For a moment they didn't speak. Then Steven told her huskily:

"You can see and know why I'm here. You been knowing how I feel about you from the first, the very first on the beach. Every time I tried to tell you before you knew it the same as if I'd said it. I'm saying it now. I been wanting you, every day, every minute. Every step I took called it out. You and the island go together, with me, all three. All I got to know from you how you look on it is one answer. I had it from Tiger that you took the other. If that's so, I want to hear you say it."

He heard her, instead, take in her breath. Slowly, staring at him with eyes wider than he had ever seen them, Adie shook her head. "Emily and Clara told Tiger to say that. They made him believe it."

Something inside him jolted so that it pained him. In trying to comprehend all things swiftly, his mind dealt first with minor matters. He stammered, "I had the idea you didn't want to see me, beyond your ma's sickness."

"You thought that up yourself, Steven."

"But you got mad when—"

"That's because I wanted us to have Hypoluxo so much."

"Then you mean you ain't taken him?"

"I've never even thought of it, Steven. And you've never seen that I haven't."

"Tiger—did you know he was going to tell me?"

"Only after he left. I hated Emily and Clara for it. Then I saw and hoped"—her words came in a bare whisper—"it would bring you sooner." She came to him. "Oh, Steven, I've waited for you to tell me. Every time you tried I had my answer ready." She came to him and gave it. "Yes, Steven, yes!"

He stood, drinking in her words and the sight of her and the feel of her so close. He didn't think when his arms went about her and he bent and their lips came together. The feathery touch came again to his mouth and then more firmly, more surely as he held her tightly.

His heart beat wildly, and he could feel hers beating as fast. He wanted to have her with him, not let her out of his sight again. He asked abruptly, "You want to come with me right now?"

Her nod answered him, telling of her willingness, her wish, like his, to delay not at all.

The door of the other room opened and her father, half-dressed, came out. In back of him was an alarmed Mrs. Titus, clad in a wrapper.

Adie let Steven tell them. Her parents, their gazes going from one to the other of them, didn't need much explanation. Her mother protested, "You can't take her like this, in the middle of the night. Even if Mrs. Paget is on the boat." For a moment Steven thought her objection might seriously interfere, until she went on, "And without any clothes or getting ready."

Adie laughed and said, "I'm ready."

Fearfully, her mother said, "I suppose you've looked after me long enough for me not to stop you in doing this." She in sisted that at least Adie have something to take with her. Adie agreed to help pack some clothes. As they went out into the other room Steven said, "There ain't much time for that."

Titus, remaining with Steven, hitched at his suspenders. His stilted manner of speaking showed emotion when he said, "Steven, I am very glad it has come out like this. Both Mrs. Titus and I were afraid that Sylvanus Hurley—"

Steven didn't waste time on that. "It's only right to tell you," he said, "that we got the county records to take back."

Titus looked pleased instead of angry. "I didn't hold with not giving them up," he said, "and few others here do. You won the election. I didn't hold with them running you out, and I don't hold with a lot that's gone on here. I would just as soon be out of the Company, too, if—"

Steven had been edging toward the door of the other room, followed by Titus. "Maybe you'll get the chance," he said.

In the other room Adie held a small carpetbag into which her mother was stuffing a last garment. Steven took the bag. Mrs. Titus said, "I don't even know how you'll be married. And I won't be there to see it."

Adie kissed her mother. They remained in each other's arms for a close moment. Then Mrs. Titus separated herself and came to Steven. Surprisingly to him, she kissed him.

Adie embraced her father, and Titus shook Steven by the hand. He seemed worried by what Steven had said, and he asked, "You're taking her right to the boat?"

"There ain't anything else worth doing right now," Steven told him.

They left by the back way. Steven held Adie's arm tightly as she lifted her skirts and they made their way to the river bank.

Tiger laughed silently at the sight of Adie. Steven handed her in the dugout, where she sat in the middle. He pushed it off the bank and climbed in himself.

They didn't use the paddles except for Tiger holding his in the water to steer. They didn't want to chance making any noise. The current carried them down the river, precisely, but not nearly fast enough.

Now that he had Adie, Steven felt the responsibility of taking her in this way. He prayed that they wouldn't be noticed while passing the trading post. From so close to it their faces could be made out in the enveloping moonlight.

At first he thought none of the sleeping forms on the shore would rouse themselves. They were nearly opposite them before one raised up. A voice called in Seminole.

Tiger didn't answer.

They drifted for another ten yards before the voice called again, louder this time.

Tiger spoke, keeping his voice low, giving it just enough volume to carry.

The Indian on the bank lay down. There was silence again on the river.

They began to leave the trading post behind when a shout came from one of its windows. It was answered by another, and then two nightshirted figures burst from the door.

Steven dug his paddle in the water, calling on Tiger to do likewise. The canoe moved ahead only at an added sluggish pace. Adie searched the bottom for another paddle. There was none. Her voice held excitement but no fright when she asked, "Do you think they'll come after us?"

"If Sylvanus saw it was you, he probably will," Steven answered. "And Bunnell will know we came for the records when he sees the sharpie."

They were halfway to the freshwater well before the two rowboats put out from the mouth of the river. These were faster than the dugout. Steven and Tiger paddled harder, heading for the well. At it they saw the sharpie's small boat, waiting for them there, from where the shore could be seen more distinctly.

Cap Jim called as they came up, "I thought I told you—"

"There ain't any time to argue," Steven said. He pulled the

boats together. To Durgan he ordered, "You get in here before Adie takes your place."

"What you—"

"Get in," Steven said. He explained as Durgan followed directions. "You and Tiger head up the bay. That'll make one of their boats follow you, giving us a better chance to get away. It wouldn't look right only one being in the canoe, and besides, there ain't room in the boat." He helped Adie into the small boat, and then climbed over into it himself.

"If you're leaving me here," Durgan complained, "how am I going to get back to the lake?"

Steven was already working an oar of the small boat. "You can come with Quimby," he said. "He'll be carrying my route from now on."

Tiger, who had caught the idea, began to paddle again, heading up the bay. Without enthusiasm, Durgan joined him.

The small boat, with the records piled under the thwarts, was loaded dangerously. Steven and Gerald worked the oars as much to keep it from being swamped as to send it through the water.

The two rowboats in pursuit separated before arriving at the well. One, containing Bunnell, went after the dugout. The other came on after the small boat, cutting across and gaining on it. In it were three men.

Cap Jim shouted to the Margaret D, to Doc, telling him to get the anchor up. Steven's hands, at the end of his oar, hit Adie's shoulder. She leaned forward, to be out of the way. From the other boat, less than a hundred yards away, there came a call, and Adie said quietly, "It's Sylvanus."

The sharpie was under slow way when they reached her side. Doc, at the tiller, gave excited directions which they didn't follow as they scrambled aboard. Linda received Adie on deck, and the three men went up after her. There was no time to take either the records or the small boat on board. Gerald carried its line to the stern, tied it there, and then took the tiller from Doc. The other boat kept coming on. It was at once evident that the Margaret D, moved by the bare breeze, could not outstrip the rowing. As if encouraged, Sylvanus, who could be made out, half-clad, working at one oar, put added effort into his rowing, and urged on the second of the beach-combers at the other oar. Standing in the prow, his arm hanging down at his side, was Theron.

Across the water Sylvanus called again. "You don't want to go with him, Adie! You don't want him!"

It was the first time Steven had heard anything frantic from the man. He realized, more fully, what Adie had come to mean to Sylvanus.

When the boat was hardly fifty yards away, Cap Jim boomed, "Keep off here! You know what's good for you, you'll keep off!"

Still the boat kept coming on, catching up with the sharpie. Theron was seen to raise his good arm. From his hand there came a puff of white smoke and then, instantly, the sound of a pistol shot rang out. The mainsail of the Margaret D gave a twitch and moonlight shone through a neat hole made in it.

Steven ducked with the others. He pushed Adie and Linda into the cockpit, ordering them to lie on the floorboards. Adie obeyed, but Linda didn't. Cap Jim roared with fury. Doc shouted from where he took refuge behind the low cabin housing. Gerald uttered Conch oaths at the tiller.

Steven darted into the cabin. From the wall he snatched the rifle. He jerked at its lever as he came out. Standing in the cockpit, with Adie at his feet, he was raising the rifle when Linda grabbed his arm.

"You don't want the blood of a man on you, boy," she said. "With me, it don't matter."

She had her hands on the rifle when Cap Jim reached them. "It's neither one of you," he told them, "as soon as I get some cartridges." He went into the cabin.

Steven saw that the rowing in the other boat had stopped.

Sylvanus was remonstrating with Theron. Now he called, "We won't shoot again. You can keep the records if you have them." Importunately, he pleaded, "I want only to talk to Adie."

Adie started to get up. "Keep down," Steven told her.

From the cockpit she called back to Sylvanus, "There's no use. I told you before."

Linda urged Steven, "I'm more rightly the one to do it—if need be." She eased the rifle out of his hands. He let her have it, not knowing why he did, but aware that Cap Jim was coming back to take it away from them both.

Linda lay prone across the deck, resting the rifle on the low rail. She fired almost immediately. Then Steven realized his mistake. Instinctively he squatted in the cockpit as Theron shot again. The bullet could be heard to thud into the side of the sharpie.

From both boats men yelled. Cap Jim came from the cabin. He ran to Linda and tried to wrench the rifle from her grasp. She wouldn't let go. Theron fired once more, missing completely. Cap Jim gave in, handing Linda a cartridge, and telling her, "Don't miss this time."

As she hurried to reload, Linda said, "I missed apurpose then, even iffen he fired the first shot afore."

Theron's fourth shot had good reason to go wild. He and Linda fired almost together. The beachcomber seemed to be hit by some quick, invisible force. It caved in his chest. Sylvanus, turned around and half-raised from his seat, was reaching for him. He missed as Theron toppled forward, out of the boat, splashing into the water and going down.

Linda called for another cartridge, crying shrilly, "Hurley had to do with Jesse, too! You give it to me!"

From Gerald there came encouraging noises. Cap Jim looked to Steven as if for his decision.

Adie, her head raised over the edge of the cockpit, breathed, "No—no, don't let her."

Steven said, "He's got enough. When he hears what the other comber told about him, he'll be leaving on the next mail boat for Key West. He'll be out of there, too, before Baker can get to him."

The Margaret D kept sailing leisurely, out of the bay and then up the glittering sea. It stopped only to take on the load from the small boat. The running lights now shone with nothing to hide, and a lamp burned in the cabin. Gerald remained at the tiller. Linda sat forward by herself, on the deck. The others left her alone.

In the cabin Doc, after shuffling among thick packets of papers, came up with a yellowed sheet. "Here's Uncle Charlie's paper. Piggott didn't have nerve enough to burn it after all." He told Steven, "With this there ain't any question of your getting Hypoluxo all according to law."

Cap Jim said to Adie, "Now we got you, what we going to do with you?" He included Steven in his question. "With the both of you?"

With a start, Steven realized he hadn't thought of that. Just to bring Adie away had been enough.

Adie had been silent since the rowboat was left behind. Now she glanced once at Steven before she had questions of her own to ask. She spoke shyly but hopefully.

"Can't a boat captain marry people?" she inquired of Cap Jim. Of Doc she wanted to know, "Aren't you county clerk now with the right to give out licenses?"

Doc looked startled. He peered above his spectacles and then began to search through the papers for the right form. Cap Jim waggled his beard and slapped his thigh a resounding crack. "By the Eternal King!" He roared with laughter. "In the morning we'll drop you on the beach off your island."

Steven stared at Adie. She gazed back, asking with her eyes if he liked her suggestions.

The thought of Jesse stole upon him. Even with its coming he knew that Jesse was the past. He was the way things happened. Adie was the future, the way things would happen, life itself.

Steven brushed each side of his mustache with one finger to try to hide a movement of his lips he was unable to control. He grinned, but with all his new bravery and ability, he couldn't trust himself to speak.